THE SOCIAL CONSTRUCTION OF CONTEXT THROUGH PLAY

M. Nawal Lutfiyya

Department of Communication
University of Louisville

UNIVERSITY
PRESS OF
AMERICA

LANHAM • NEW YORK • LONDON

British Cataloging in Publication Information Available

Library of Congress Cataloging-in-Publication Data

Lutfiyya, M. Nawal, 1956-
The social construction of context through play.

Bilbiography: p.
Includes index.
1. Communication—Social aspects. 2. Social
interaction. 3. Symbolic interactionism. 4. Context
(Lingusitics) 5. Play. I. Title.
HM258.L88   1987   302.2   86-33959
ISBN 0-8191-6134-9 (alk. paper)
ISBN 0-8191-6135-7 (pbk. : alk. paper)

All University Press of America books are produced on acid-free
paper which exceeds the minimum standards set by the National
Historical Publication and Records Commission.

To my parents, Billie Mae Voss (1930-1977)
and
Abdullah Mohamed Lutfiyya (1929-1977)

ACKNOWLEDGEMENTS

No work is ever completed without the help of others and I have had my share of concerned and helpful people without which whom this work would never have been completed.

My intellectual indebtedness to Carl Couch and Dan E. Miller is greater than I can express. Dan E. Miller introduced me to sociological and theoretical questions which transformed my understanding of the world. Carl Couch helped to further my theoretical stance in the world. I continue to admire both their commitment to sociology and their sociological endeavors.

Jane Blankenship, Vernon Cronen, and Jack Hewitt were members of my dissertation committee while I was a student at the University of Massachusetts at Amherst. I was especially fortunate to have worked with them and remain thankful to them for their time and willingness to share their knowledge.

The actual study conducted could not have been completed without the consent and efforts of Fern Johnson, Marlene G. Fine, and M. Sallyanne Ryan. Not only did they allow me to work with them on research regarding women`s perceptions of communication but they allowed me to videotape our working together and to study our playing together.

Sue Lawrence and David McCraw volunteered their time as reliability coders. Barbara J. Wilson and James P. Dillard collaborated their efforts in finding a last minute statistic for my analysis. While Barbara Lavin, Bob Lewis and Nadine Foley provided comfort and support during many trying months. Their efforts are greatly appreciated.

Fern Johnson poured through numerous writings and re-writings of this work. Further, she provided comfort, support and encouragement to complete this project when I was more than willing to let the whole thing go. Any way you choose to slice up life, she's the best.

My siblings Jad Jamil, Zana Marie, and Sami David and my family of friends Lee Malcolmson, Barbara

Carson, Bruce Mac Murray, Susan Frankel and Don Markley offered their continuous inspiration, support and friendship.

Lastly, I owe a great deal to Carolyn Anderson. Not only is she a friend but she is a role model. When I grow-up I want to be like Carolyn.

TABLE OF CONTENTS

ix

LIST OF TABLES

LIST OF ILLUSTRATIONS

C H A P T E R   O N E

INTRODUCTION

> Without context, words and actions
> have no meaning at all. This is
> true not only of human
> communication in words but also of
> all communication whatsoever, of
> all mental processes, of all mind..
> . . (Bateson, 1972:482)

The Research Question

The primary question guiding the present
investigation is: How are communicative contexts
created? Since all human communication is social in
nature a functionally equivalent question is: How are
social contexts created? This question and its answers
are central to, at the very least, human communication
theory specifically and the endeavor of social science
and investigative research in general. While this work
focuses on the first issue---human communication
theory, in this introductory chapter I will comment on
both these issues. Three additional themes are
introduced in this chapter in order to aquaint the
reader with the issues focused upon in the next three
chapters. Addressed first is context as meaning
creation. This topic is the major focus of chapter
two. Play as the research site for generating data to
answer the question of context creation is the second
issue. It is discussed as "fanciful recontextualization" and is given full attention in chapter three.
Last, the methodology and methods employed for the
study are introduced. These are the foci for the
fourth chapter.

Context As Meaning Creation

Not only is all human behavior contextualized
(Bateson, 1972) or bracketed (Garfinkle, 1967) but for
any human to act in or on the world meaning must be
made of the world and objects in it; humans, afterall,
are symbolic by nature. As Stone and Faberman (1970)
state it: "Man is nothing without symbols. The very

fact that man must use symbols to define the situations in which he conducts himself implies communication, since those very definitions require the meaningful response of others" (p.148). It is this meaning or sense which provides the brackets or containers within which the world of "wide-wake practical realities" (Schutz, 1966) are created and unfold. Ultimately, meaning cannot exist separate of context, while context is possible because human beings create meaning. The relationship between context and meaning is reflexive¹.

While grappling with the processes of meaning and contexting, Goffman (1973) introduces the term "framework" as a conceptual merger of meaning creation and contextualization. Goffman (1973) then distinguishes between "primary frameworks" and all others with "keying" as the behavioral and conceptual transformer. Keying involves a systematic transformation in meaning assigned to behavior or action. Goffman (1973) suggests that keying cues participants to interpret behavior from a primary framework different than what would ordinarily be used. Keying, for example, allows for the interpretation of "playing at fighting" versus "fighting". Primary frameworks are those "cultural" understandings or assumptions operating when members of the same culture interact with one another. In many ways these primary frameworks remain outside the critical consciousness of everyday interactants. When describing primary frameworks Goffman (1973) offers:

> When the individual in our Western society recognizes a particular event, he tends, whatever else he does, to imply in this response (and in effect employ) one or more frameworks or schemata of interpretation of a kind that can be called primary. . . . (A) primary framework is one that is seen as rendering what would otherwise be a meaningless aspect of the scene into something that is meaningful. . . . (E)ach primary framework allows its user to locate, perceive, identify, and label a seemingly infinite number

2

of concrete occurences defined in
its terms (p.21).

Goffman then proceeds to distinguish between two
"types" of primary frameworks: natural and social.
This distinction is an important one because it
introduces "social frameworks" as inherently
communicative, where the creation and necessary
maintenance of these are a process of communication.

Natural and Social Frameworks

Natural frameworks, accordingly, are purely
physical and as Goffman (1973) describes them are
exemplified as the focus of biological inquiry. Since
natural frameworks are purely physical they are
undirected ". . . no actor continuously guides the
outcome" (p. 22). Human "sexual drive peaks" serve as
illustration of natural frameworks. As a naturally
occuring phenomena human males and females reach peaks
in their sexual drives at different times, males during
late adolesence and females during their middle
fourties.

Social frameworks, by contrast, are "guided
doings". This second type of framework involves the
elements of motive and intent and provides a background
understanding of events that incorporate the
controlling effort of an intelligence, a human being.
Finally, Goffman (1973) makes the observation that ". .
. all social frameworks involve rules. . ." (p.24);
humanly constructed rules. While determinism prevails
with natural frameworks, with social frameworks the
willful agency of human action (and interactivity)
prevails. General courting and mating patterns of
Western cultures illustrates social frameworks.
For instance, part of the courting ritual of
heterosexuals in Western cultures includes the dictum
that the male be older or at least not younger in age
than the female. Thus while biologically or
"naturally" occuring frames impose different sexual
drive peak time ' frames on men and women, socially
constructed frames guide mating and courting behavior
in ways which "get over" or at the very least modify
the natural.

Even though Goffman (1973) differentiates natural
and social frameworks from one another, he does comment
on their "overlapping." Indeed it is foolhardy to
suggest that the two do not have an impact on one
another. As Goffman aptly observes: ". . .whatever an
agent seeks to do will be continuously conditioned by
natural constraints. . ." (p. 23). Thus, he continues,
". . .although natural events occur without intelligent
intervention, intelligent doings cannot be accomplished
effectively without entrance into the natural order"
(p. 23). To return one last time to the courting and
mating example consider the following twist. While
biologically or naturally human males and females
reach peaks in their sexual drive at different ages and
while the social frame of courting and mating modifies
the naturally occuring differences, the constructed
social frame may indeed be constructed around yet
another simultaneously occuring natural frame. Human
males remain fertile longer than human females, hence,
when the "socially desireable" age differences are
created and acted upon, males are courting and mating
with females who have more child-bearing years than
females who are either the same age as the male or
older than the male. (I am presuming, of course, that
fertility is an issue).

This overlapping of natural and social contexts
involves what Mead (1934) calls a process of
"adjustment." Language use and significant symbols
facilitates this adjustment process. In Miller's
(1973) words:

> Language or significant symbols are
> for the purpose of facilitating the
> process of adjustment, and they
> enter into the process when social
> acts cannot be completed
> satisfactorily by a duplication or
> repitition of one's prior action,
> when the act cannot be carried out
> by the application of habits alone
> (p. 75).

While natural frameworks or contexts are
determined by habits alone, social frames or contexts
are created by the use of language or significant
symbols. These social contexts, then, become
communicative in the sense that they, once established,

4

impinge on (but do not determine) ongoing talk and interaction. Social contexts which impinge on talk suggest that communication is context-dependent. Cronen and Lannamann (1981: 3) point out that the context-dependence of communication is not only well-documented but, "the current evidence for the context dependence of communication has far-reaching implications for our field." Once context-dependence has been acknowledged we must ask: "Where do contexts come from?" Cronen and Lannamann (1981:4) continue: "The long-range import of the context dependent view rests on the ability of communication theory to account for the creation of context."

Language Use and Context Creation

From an interactionist standpoint, social context must be understood as phenomena constructed by human beings largely through discourse and always through communication. From Mead (1934) onward, symbolic interactionists have maintained that human beings continually use communication to create and transform complex worlds of interaction (Stone and Faberman, 1970; and Maines, 1977). As Duncan (1962) notes:

> Few social theorists have made communication so central to their systems as Mead. Indeed, it may be said that his theory of society is based on a theory of communication. Even our knowledge of external nature is determined by our social experience in communication.

Interactionists who remain true to their theory begin and end with interaction and communication. For Mead (1934) and later Wittgenstein (1957, 1958) language use is communication. Miller (1973) in pointing out the similarity in the positions of Mead and Wittgenstein notes that both share the belief that "private language" does not exist and that communication and meaning are reliant upon the use of "significant symbols" (p. 70). In fact the terms "private language" and "significant symbols" are conceptually opposites. For Wittgenstein a "private language" would be a symbol system peculiar to an

5

individual alone. "Significant symbols", on the other hand, are communication since they arouse in the other the same response as the self.

By tying meaning to discourse and communication, the claim ultimately becomes that the social context for interpreting meaning is also tied to the ongoing discourse. Social context is both socially constructed and fluid. Neither Mead nor Wittgenstein carry through to specify how contexts are created. As Perinbanayagam (1974) states regarding Wittgenstein's work: "For Wittgenstein. . . a mere assertion that meaning arises out of social process, out of life forms, is perhaps adequate. But, it is important to specify the nature of the process and demonstrate how a mutuality of perspectives is possible and how common usages begin to occur" (p.525). Both Mead and Wittgenstein indicate, however, that the importance of understanding social context and specifically the process of contextualization underlies the crucial idea that human beings possess the constructionary powers to do things rather than merely have things happen. Language use, according to Mead (1934), provides the constructionary powers since it is the use of language which allows humans to envision futures and thereby break out of inevitably specific responses in redundant social situations. The process of breaking out of redundant meaning or response patterns results in new contexts for interpreting behavior.

In the exploratory work described in this book, I will emphasize the idea of contextualization, or the active and interactive creation of context as key to some of the complextities of human interaction and communicative behavior. As already established, human interaction and communicative behavior are the focus of inquiry for symbolic interactionists. As such, the premises of symbolic interaction theory underlie this investigation. A triangulated data generation technique is employed by combining the methods of ethnography, videotaping the naturally occuring interaction, and participant observation. As a data generation technique, ethnography, deserves special attention here because of its unique tie to the issue of context. The next section addresses this connection.

6

Context and Social Science Research

In general, attempting to delineate the actual process of contextualization using social science research methods introduces yet another twist to the overall question of context creation. Afterall, social scientists who quest for universal statements about certain features of social life are continually confronted with the intriguing notion of context. More specifically, social scientists who maintain that their task is to generate and delineate rules of behavior which stand free of context ^{2} are nevertheless faced with the challenge to demonstrate that their findings ". . . apply over and over again in many different contexts" (Watzlawick, Beavin and Jackson, 1967: 70). Likewise, external validity, one bastion of the scientific method requires that the contexts which bind any research finding be identified.

Ethnography entails the "description and analysis of human behavior based on a long term observational study on the spot" (Heider, 1976). The analysis of ethnographic data must include the attempt to relate "specific observed behavior to cultural norms" (Heider, 1976). In other words the data must be put into a cultural context. The goals of ethnographic research makes ethnographic researchers sensitive to the issue of context. And as Trueba (1982) points out, the meaning and use of the concept "context" in ethnographic research has become so controversial that some ethnographers have divided into the camps of micro-ethnographers and macro-ethnographers (p.22). This controversy hinges on conceptualizations of contextualization and decontextualization. To this regard Trueba (1982) argues that if context ". . . is a set of cues that permit us to situate and interpret the localized meanings of interactional exchanges" (p. 26), then contextualization is a process that "leads to a global and cohesive interpretation of behavior" (p. 26). By extension decontextualization is a process of detaching the immediate social, historical, economic, educational, and political surroundings from the behavior being examined.

Macro-ethnographers, as Trueba (1982) describes them, argue that the appropriate context of a valid ethnography is holistic and encompassing. Further, they argue that: "their concerns for the cultural

7

imperatives and broader historical sociopolitical issues are a sine qua non for interpreting interaction in more specific settings" (p. 23).

In contrast to macro-ethnography, micro-ethnography is by definition an effort to make social scientific findings useful and applicable to real-life problems as these arise in very specific and situated contexts. Clearly, the concerns of macro and micro-ethnography appear to be in conflict. Thus, even though micro-ethnographers accept the reasoning of macro-ethnography they rejoin that ethnographic research cannot stay at the general level and they, in general, state that: "micro-ethnographic research will continue to be a productive endeavor even in instances where contextualization does not satisfy ethnography requirements" (p.23).

While Trueba (1982) himself argues that the dichotomy is "artificial and unwarranted" in that the positions are actually complementary and not different; the fact that the dichotomy exists at all indicates the importance of "context" to the endeavor of doing social science. Ultimately, validating ethnographic description is dependent upon the use of appropriate contextual cues allowing the researcher to make legitimate inferences thus understanding the behavior observed. In describing this process, Trueba (1982) explains:

> Context, both in micro and macro ethnographic approaches, is meant to provide cues for the selection of relevant features of behavior vis-a-vis specific conceptual frames. Contextualization, therefore, follows a body of theory and a set of theoretical principles. Decontextualization, on the other hand, occurs at all levels of research endeavors from the data gathering and data configurations, to the analysis of interaction exchanges, or to broader contextualization of societal trends, structures, and values, and ultimately, to a theory of behavior"(p.21).

8

Essentially, then, in doing research about context and the process of contextualization one must "know" the context within which contextualization is studied. Afterall, once humans become language users and once human sociation, societies, and cultures become language-dependent a "context" free social environment cannot exist.

Thus, while the term context possesses the denotative meaning "to weave together," the concept must inevitably be tied to phenomena which are or can be woven. Futhermore, when the term "social" precedes context, a suggestion is made that human actors are in some way the weavers. For my study I assume: 1) that contexts are created by human actors, and 2) that contexts are social in nature. In other words, it is through communication that contexts are created and, by extension, transformed as well as shared.

In addressing the issue of "phenomena which are or can be woven" in the creation of contexts, a handful of social scientists have suggested that play and context go hand in hand (cf. Bateson, 1972; Simmel, 1950; and Duncan, 1962). Playing, therefore, is a useful example of interaction that can be analyzed to answer the question: "How are contexts created?" Play, it is argued has no meaning apart from communicative contexts because when people play with one another, they "communicate a play intention" (Bateson, 1972). This play intention involves the explicit signalling of a transformation in the interpretive framework for what the behavior means. In other words, communicating the play intention is an alchemic moment where the intrinsic and extrinsic change places, where the serious is subordinated to the non-serious.

Recapitulation

What is proposed, then, as a step toward understanding social context is to focus on the process of contextualizing certain behaviors. With human play as a research site the focus is not simply on contextualizing but on re-contextualizing. In this light, play and context are conceptually merged. The following section outlines this conceptual merger.

9

Context and Play as Fanciful
Recontextualization

As Bateson (1972), Simmel (1950) and Duncan (1962, 1968) suggest, an understanding of play is possible only if play is studied and examined in relation to social context; in particular the creation of context or the transformation of context. In some ways I have flipped this suggestion around. For my purposes, context will be understood through the analysis of play.

Bateson (1972) writes that researching play illuminates the human process of metacommunication (communicating about communication). Meta-communication involves the recognition of signs as signals. Reference is to the denotative messages emergent in interaction. In contexts established as playful, where the message "this is play" is conveyed, the signals implicitly denote what would ordinarily be explicit signals such as threat or anger. The implied denotation carries a negation of the explicit. Bateson (1972:180), thus, posits this definition of play: ". . . The actions in which we now engage, do not denote what would be denoted by those actions which these actions denote." According to Bateson, in a playful situation the literalness or seriousness of the message is transformed and not meant as it might be ordinarily.

Simmel (1950) and Duncan (1962, 1968) in a similar vein, observe that play transforms the serious as play activity is connected to conceptualizations of form and content. In this regard Simmel (1950) argues that the play form emerges from the contents of ordinary or serious life situations, but ultimatley is not bound in these contents. Play as a transformational process, develops an "autonomous existence" (Simmel, 1950).

This transformational nature of play, the ability of play to re-define ongoing serious activity, is what ties playing to contextualization. To conceptually merge the study of context creation and play I have adopted from Katovich (1979) the term "Fanciful Recontextualization" . Briefly, the term "Fanciful Recontextualization" denotes playful activity as a social act (as Mead, 1934, defines social act) which

10

everyday or serious life situations. Transforming the contents of the ongoing production of ordinary life in a playful manner creates new social relationships as well as new consequences for interaction. I will explore this further in a later section of the book. For now, the introduction of play, provides a starting point for answering questions about context creation. Play, as a research site grounds the question of context creation to observable social action[4].

Once context creation or contextualization has been "grounded," two concerns must be addressed: 1) what constitutes context (as opposed to the actual process of contextualization)? and 2) what actually is the observable social action of playing and re-contextualizing? Addressing the first concern provides groundwork for addressing the second.

Constituent Elements of Context

Six aspects of context have been identified from the literature: consequences of behavior, subjective interpretation, shared language, boundaries of interaction, systemic qualities and reflexivity. While no single work deals comprehensively with these aspects, each piece of literature reviewed contributes to what might become a comprehensive theory of social context. At this point I will briefly introduce the germane elements of context since chapter two is an extensive discussion of context.

Social Consequences

Thomas and Swaine Thomas (1928) and Cronen and Lannamann (1981) deal specifically with this issue. When human beings interact with one another, when we talk and produce social realities, our behaviors are consequential. Interaction is consequential since meaning is attributed to it. Mead (1934) claims that meaning and therefore consequence, lies in the response of one person to anothers actions. Not too differently, Thomas and Swaine Thomas (1928) argue that if something is real it is real in its consequences.

11

Subjective Interpretation

Meaning and consequence are possible because of subjective interpretation or minded behavior (Mead, 1934). Subjective interpretation is the second constitutive element of context. What constitutes minded behavior remains debateable in social science circles, however, Whorf (1956) and Mead (1934) persuasively argue that the minded behavior of interpretation is bound by and in shared language.

Shared Language

The concern of shared language and situation as discussed by Malinowski (1923), Whorf (1956) and Mead (1934) is the third dimension of context I have identified from the context and situated activity literature. Their arguments, while not mirror images of one another, offer that for persons to identify objects in the world and to make decisions about how to act on those objects, a process of objectification or naming must take place. This process of language creation culminates in interpretive frameworks.

Boundaries

Boundaries are conceptualized in either very structural and concrete terms as evidenced in Goffman's (1963) work or in abstract terms as found in Mead's (1934) social act.

While ultimately I intend to provide an empirically based model of contextualization, human interaction which contextualizes always occur in some sort of boundary or situation. In one of his earlier pieces, Goffman (1963) grapples with the issue of the boundary of human sociation within the rubric of "social occasion." Goffman was writing about the broader frame of reference in which situated activity takes place. The concept of social occasion is presented as a wide context within which persons are able to become oriented to one another. The boundary is:

> ". . . a wider social affair, undertaking, or event, bounded in regard to place and time and typically facilitated by fixed equipment; a social occasion provides the structuring context in

12

which many situations or gatherings
are likely to form, dissolve, and
reform, while a pattern of conduct
tends to be recognized as the
appropriate and (often) official
or intended one..."(1963:18).

On a continuum, boundaries vary from the very
structural to the very fluid, or, in Goffman's
(1963:198-215) terms, from the very tight to the very
loose. He states: "We usually think of tight occasions
as ones in which the participants have many onerous
situational obligations, and loose contexts as ones
relatively free of those constraints" (1963:207).

Systemic Qualities

The systemic conceptualization of the Palo Alto
group or cybernetic theory can be discussed in terms of
Glasser and Strauss's (1967), Stover's (1974),
Watzlawick, et al.'s (1967) and Bateson's (1972)
informational bias.

Within boundaried situations, interactants who
have and use a shared symbol system create and transmit
information. Cybernetic theory deals with the
transmission of information or communication and
Watzlawick, et al. (1967) argue that since humans are
communicating beings then a cybernetic model adequately
describes human social behavior (as communication and
behavior are viewed as one and the same). Shibutani
(1968) and Stover (1974) observe that ". . . the
original symbolic interactionist theory of Mead and
Dewey incorporated a crude cybernetic theory of
human behavior" (Stover, 1974:7). In this light,
Stover (1974:9) defines context as ". . . all features
of a situation external to or supra to a given
interaction sequence (ie. the actual fitting together
of behaviors) which canalize behavior into particular
forms of association. . . . The context specifies (by
the information it imparts to the interactants) the
variety of behaviors possible in a given situation"
(Stover, 1974:9).

What is suggested, then, is that social context be
understood as information contexts, where ". . . every
social context can. . . be resolved into myriad
contexts or patterns of messages which exist at various

13

levels of abstraction" (Stover, 1974:10). Higher levels of abstraction provide information on behavioral choices at lower levels. Contexts of information are, thus, hierarchically arranged.

Reflexivity

Even though any notion of context implies a hierarchy, few conceptualizations introduce reflexivity between levels as important. Watzlawick, et al. (1967), associate reflexivity with confusion, thus positing reflexivity as problematic. On the other hand, Cronen and Lannamann (1981) offer that a notion of reflexivity is essential if communication theory is to account for the creation of context through talk ". . . as well as for the way context exerts effects on the process of the talk itself" (p.4). According to Cronen and Lannamann (1981), "reflexivity exists whenever two elements in a hierarchical system are organized so that each is simultaneously context for and contexted by the other" (p.1). Not too differently from Cronen and Lannamann (1981) Burke's (1945) dramatistic consideration of ratios emergent from his analytical pentad is an effort to describe "the container and the thing contained" (p.3) in social action.

Briefly, to analyze instances of reciprocal activity or sociality embodying human motivation, Burke offers a pentad made-up of act, scene, agent, agency, and purpose.

> In a rounded statement about motives, you must have some word that names the act (names what took place in thought or deed), another that names the scene (the background of the act), the situation in which it occured; also you must indicate what persons or kinds of persons (agent) performed the act, what means or instruments he used (agency), and the purpose (Burke, 1945:XV).

14

In essence this pentad treats language and thought as modes of action. From the five key terms of dramatism, ten possible ratios are allowed.

The scene-act ratio and the act-agency ratio are the most interesting to a discussion of context. Regarding the scene-act ratio Burke (1945:3) states:

> Using 'scene' in the sense of setting, or background, and 'act' in the sence of actions, one could say that the scene contains the act. And using the agents in the sense of actors, or acters, one could say that the scene contains the agents.

Burke (1945:16) describes the act-agency ratio as:

> the agent does not contain the act, though its results might be said to pre-exist virtually within him. And the act does not synecdochially share in the agent, though certain ways of acting may be said to induce corresponding modes or traits of character. . . . The act-agency ratio more strongly suggests a temporal or sequential relationship than a purely positional or geometric one. The agent is the author of his own acts, which are descended from him, being good progeny if he be good, bad progeny if he is bad. . . . And conversely, his acts can make or remake him in accordance with their nature. They would be his product and/or he would be theirs.

Even the most explicit categorically defined situations or ritualized acts are continually subtended by a process of social interaction; this process invites a change in as well as maintains that which is salient. When human beings play, the ensuing interaction, while situated, changes the context of the interaction. The meaning of behaviors change. In other words, acts staged by actors challenge scenes. Likewise, when actors are agents, the acts are not only

15

actor created but the created acts form a reflexive relationship and eventually impinge upon the actors. Acts are not the sum total of agents.

An Example of Fanciful Recontextualization: "Misterhood is Powerful"

While the conversational data analyzed for this research is, in part, analyzed with a Burkean perspective additional analytical frames are also used. However, to illustrate fanciful recontextualization more concretely, the following example is presented from a Burkean point of view. Not only, however, is Burke's notion of reflexivity incorporated into this brief illustrative example but the five other dimensions of context are also noted.

A real-life situation reported in The Boston Phoenix illustrates fanciful recontextualization. On April 12, 1982, The Boston Phoenix reported that "about thirty members of the Ladies Against Women (LAW) a self-described 'natural branch of the ladies non-movement' donned white gloves and hats for a trip to MIT's Kresge Auditorium to demonstrate at a debate between Decrow and Shafley" (The Boston Phoenix, April 12, 1982). Not only were "neat, polite press releases" made, but the crowd demonstrating carried signs with the slogans: "Roses not Raises," "Sperm are People Too," "Tupperware, not Welfare," "Forced Pregnancy Increases Church Membership," and "Misterhood is Powerful." In the press releases, Saundra Stephen, local LAW vice-chairman, was quoted as saying that even though Phyllis Shafley was not a stay-at-home woman who was spending all of her time raising children and such, she nevertheless ". . . always thanks her husband Fred for allowing her to come," presumably to the public meetings she so frequently attends. Another LAW member was quoted to say:

> It's so thrilling to have a visit from someone like Mrs. Shafley, who represents everything that women should stand for- - - militarism, racism, true religion, and women's submission (The Boston Phoenix, April 12, 1982).

Although on the surface it may first appear that this public demonstration was serious, it becomes clear that it was not; the "real" organization sponsoring the demonstration was "The Coalition for Reproductive Freedom." Moreover, the slogans used were plays on Feminist slogans. Instead of actually conducting a "serious" demonstration, this particular organization had the foresight to "stage" a playful demonstration which recontextualized the serious in such as way as to comment on the occurrence of Phyllis Shafley making a public appearance.

For the LAW group to make an impact as intended, to be consequential, they were reliant on the subjective interpretation of others. While a shared language is essential for any communication to occur, a particular informational bias had to be in operation for the message to be understood. This informational bias is connected with and, in part, made possible by the "boundaries" of the interaction episode or, in Burkean terms, the scene. It is the interplay between the scene and the act, the scene-act ratio, which establishes the informational bias.

In the LAW episode there is an act within an act which is initially contained by a scene but which eventually contains the scene. While Burke (1945) discusses scene-act ratios in a more clear-cut fashion, he does offer that: ". . . any act could be treated as part of the context that modifies (hence, to a degree motivates) the subsequent acts" (p.7).

In the episode being analyzed, the simultaneous acts are: 1) the debate, and 2) the demonstration. The first act, obviously, motivated the second. The contemporary political situation of women in$_5$ the United States provided the scene. Womanists who have taken particular standpoints (shared standpoints) on the current political situation of woman in America were the agents in the episode. Play or fanciful recontextualization emerged as the agency or the instrument facilitating the act and facilitating the act containing the scene. Finally, the purpose of the demonstration was to challenge, make a comment on, and make explicit opposing standpoints. The demonstration not only makes a comment on the debate in light of the contemporary political situation of women in the United States, but the demonstration, because of its fanciful essence which recontextualizes, encompasses the scene and therefore becomes momentarily the political situation of women in the United States.

Just as the scene contains the two identified acts creating the scene-act ratio, an agent-act ratio is also emergent. Demonstrating (act) by LAW members (agents) is what fancifully recontextualizes the debate gathering and gathers. The act-agent ratio is reflexive and the action creates something which stands over and above any individual or the sum of the collective. How that "recontextualized context" comes to stand over and above those who create it, while it is being created, is the process that the empirical investigation at hand will specify. This process is constituted by a sequence of acts characterized by mutuality. The next section, Methodology, will clarify both what this type of process is as well as how it will be investigated.

Methodology

Data Generation and Sampling

While the general research site for this study is spontaneously emerging adult play, a social situation for the generation of researchable data had to be selected which both generated manageable data and maintained the integrity of the spontaneity of play. This was obtained through naturalistic inquiry by combining three qualitative data generation procedures: ethnography; videotaping naturally occuring social interaction; and participant observation. Combining these methods culminated in triangulated data generation (Denzin, 1970:26-27).

Using a stationary camera, a task-oriented, small group was videotaped over the total time of five hours. The time frame emerged naturally and was based on the time required for a research team to complete their task. These five hours were not continuous.

The naturally formed group was a research team of four womanists conducting research on women's perceptions of their own communication. All five hours videotaped consisted of the collective task of content analyzing responses to open-ended survey questions.

Transcripts (see Appendix A) were made of the "playful" episodes which emerged during the videotaping. Both the transcripts and the video recordings were analyzed in regard to the research question. Through the use of theoretical sampling (Glasser and Strauss, 1967: 45-77) a constant mapping of data to theory was accomplished. A desirable sample, as we all know, is one that mirrors as nearly as possible the total population. As Glaser and Strauss (1967) describe the process of theoretical sampling, sampling does not end until a completely grounded theory is developed. These authors argue a logic of ongoing inclusion that dictates that successive sampling from relevant events must be employed. In this regard a fluid interactive relationship exists between theory and sampling. For this study the population consists of all instances of play which emerged during the taped interaction. To accomplish theoretical sampling all instances of the data were analyzed to discover the process of context creation.

The analysis of video recorded interaction combines the empirical techniques of naturalistic inquiry and repeated observation with theory construction. These analytical techniques enhance one another, overcoming problems inherent in each of the individual techniques. Once social interaction has been aurally and visually recorded, it becomes "re-searchable" data. It is from the redundant observation of the same frozen slices of social life that theory is generated and not from fieldnotes, which traditionally are the data of naturalistic inquiry. "Searching" and "researching" fieldnotes twice removes the theorist from the actual instances of social life being analyzed. Ultimately the fieldnotes are being analyzed.

Videotaping, typically, is used in experimental or laboratory settings where the objects of investigation are strangers (to the researcher and theorist). The special privileges which accompany the status of "knowledgable participant," then are denied the researcher. Important information, consequentially, is lost. Access to this type of special information is possible once the researcher becomes part subject and object of the investigation. Video-recordings enhance naturalistic inquiry when a knowledgable participant observer is also involved in the research endeavor.

19

Even though theoretical sampling is integral to the process of theory generation; the collection, coding and analysis of the data are not simultaneous activities as they are in the procedure of Grounded Theory which is typically associated with theoretical sampling (Glasser and Strauss, 1967). The coding and analysis of the data, however, are simultaneous and dynamic activities.

Data Analysis and Theory Construction

While a thorough discussion of the analysis appears in chapter four, another aspect of these procedures warrants mention: the inductive nature of the data analysis and theory construction. Since my intention is to develop a theory of contextualization based on empirical observations, no hypotheses will be tested as usually are in deductive endeavors.

Research always begins with the formulation of a theoretical question. Pre-conceptualizations about observable behaviors are involved in theoretical questions. The statement of a theoretical problem marks the initiation of a scientific endeavor. Mead (1936:281) stated:

> It is well to recognize that observation is not simply an opening of one's eyes and seeing what there is about or opening one's ears and listening to what may occur. It is always directed by some sort of a problem which lies back in one's mind; it always expresses an interest of some sort.

The researcher, thus, performs a theoretical act by formulating a question and by selecting a research site.

While questions are theoretically guided, they are not chained to preconceptualizations. The sophistication of theoretical concepts at the initial stage of the research must not be formidable. Further, the inductive researcher makes the commitment to not let any previously formed or established idea supplant

20

the data. In fact, objectionable facts, negative cases, or those data which do not conform to preconceptions and reconceptions are sought out. Hence, the degree of specificity of the theoretical concepts increases throughout the research process. Negative cases or all instances of the data are included in the theoretical scheme as it is refined. In this way generic social processes (to the data at hand) are "discovered" from the data.

After deciding to conduct empirical analysis and once a research site has been selected, theoretical premises supply a framework around which definitive concepts can develop. On this issue, Blumer (1969) is informative. While Mead (1936) argues that the research endeavor begin with a question, Blumer (1969) offers that observation is preferable. As starting points the stands are incompatible, however, as separate points in the research, they are not. "How" to look, as depicted by Mead (1936), is fundamental for subsequent theory construction just as observation and articulation, as depicted by Blumer (1969) are foremost in empirical investigation. Blumer (1969:7) avers:

> A cardinal principle of symbolic interactionism is that any empirically oriented scheme of human society, however derived, must respect the fact that in the first and last instance human society consists of people engaging in action. To be empirically valid the scheme must be consistent with the nature of the social action of human beings.

In developing a methodology of symbolic interactionism, Blumer (1969) applies Mead's concept of social action to empirical investigations. This application specifies the nature and use of the concept, and by renaming the concept "joint action," Blumer refers to it as "the larger collective form of action that is constituted by the fitting together of the lines of behavior of the separate participants" (1969:70). As Blumer then continues, when organizing observations and constructing theories of social activity, joint action is the simplest unit of

21

analysis. I argue that joint action is the simplest
unit of <u>communicative analysis</u>.

As a scientific enterprise, symbolic
interactionism, is concerned with more than describing
reciprocal acts, it is concerned with the ordering of
events (Mead, 1934, 1936). To this end, the concept of
joint action is expanded to social process. Social
process is the temporal organization of a series of
joint actions. As a consequence, the processual
organization of observations of joint action provides
one of the necessary guidelines for the analysis of
video-recordings to generate scientific statements.
Social forms is yet another theoretical premise which
guides the arrangement of data. Using Simmel's "forms
of association" (1950) the researcher selects research
sites where the participants' have organized ways of
relating to one another which have formal level
similarities across various contents; i.e., the
participants are engaged in egalitarian relationships
or boss-worker relationships. As such the researcher
uses "social relationship" concepts to describe and
compare coordinated behavior that occurs when people
interact with one another. The translation of social
behavior into explicit formal categories is
accomplished by the combination of observation of
behavior and the commitment to describing those
behaviors as social forms. As Duncan (1969) phrases it:
"If we say that symbolic action takes place in forms,
the forms of interaction in society we call
communication, what is the structure of such action?"
(Duncan, 1969: 203).

In short, the social scientist concludes her
research with statements of uniformities, and the
researcher and theorist organizes her behavior to
achieve this goal. By anticipating generic social
process, the researcher begins with a theoretically
guided generic question, in this paper the original
question is: How are social contexts created? and it is
theoretically transformed into: What is the structured
process of context creation. This is the question
which remains throughout the research process.

In light of the theoretically guided research
procedures, the theory constructed in this work is
intended to be a contribution to a particular class of
theory: interpretive social theory characterized by

non-positivistic meta-theory. In the final analysis I will be endeavoring to do more; in particular I attempt to merge the findings of this analysis with the concerns of critical theory. I will briefly elaborate.

Recently, interpretive theorizing has been contrasted to critical theorizing (Fay, 1976). Noteworthy among the distinctions is the endeavor of critical theorists to uncover both the manifest and latent aspects of human social life and the structural artifacts of social interaction. Critical theorists claim that interpretive theorists uncover and explain only manifest aspects. While the research is guided by interpretive social theory, it is my intention to discuss the implications of this research within a critical domain. This discussion will occur in the final chapter of the book.

Forecast

This book has five more chapters. Chapter two presents a theory of contextualization. Pertinent literature is reviewed and synthesized. The third chapter is an extended discussion of fanciful recontextualization. Not only is the literature on play reviewed but a hierarchical framework of fanciful recontextualization is also presented. Methodology and methods are discussed in chapter four and the results and analysis are presented in the fifth chapter. Last, the final chapter discusses the results of this study in a critical framework. This critical framework offers an approach for future research.

Endnotes

1. According to Cronen and Lannamann (1981), "reflexivity exists whenever two elements in a hierarchical system are organized so that each is simultaneously context for and contexted by the other" (p.1). Further, these authors offer that a notion of reflexivity is essential if communication theory is to account for the creation of context through talk, ". . .as well as for the way context exerts effects on the process of talk itself" (p.4).

2. Labov and Fanshell's work on Therapeutic Discourse is an attempt to discover rules of behavior that stand free of context.

3. This term was first suggested by Michael Katovich in his M.A. thesis Play. Fanciful recontextualization was a term he used to describe a particular type of play. While we do not use the term in the same way, he has given me permission to use the term Fanciful Recontextualization.

4. While play grounds the question of context to observable social behavior by allowing the researcher to study how recontextualization takes place, it would be a mistake to assume that it is the only place to observe this activity. Clearly, Bormann's work on fantasy theme analysis is an attempt to study recontextualization.

5. This term is used intentionally, it is not a typo. In her book In Search Of Our Mothers' Gardens, Alice Walker introduces the term "womanist." While she delineates four definitions for this term, only the last three apply here and throughout the book. These definitions are:

> 2. Also: A woman who loves other women, sexually and/or nonsexually. Appreciates and prefers women's culture, women's emotional flexibility (values tears as natural counterbalance of laughter),and women's strength. Sometimes loves individual men, sexually and/or nonsexually. Committed to survival and wholeness of entire people, male and female. Not a separatist, except periodically, for health. . . .

24

3. Loves music. Loves dance. Loves the moon.
Loves the Spirit. Loves love and food and roundness.
Loves struggle. Loves the Folk. Loves herself.
Regardless.
4. Womanist is to feminist as purple to
lavender (Walker, 1983:xi-xii).

CHAPTER TWO

THEORY OF CONTEXT

> (S)ocial theorists frequently
> testify to the significance of
> context, but have rarely provided
> precise definitions of it or
> descriptions of the contextualizing
> function. . . .(Branham and Pearce,
> 1985)

Framing the Issues

Many students of human behavior would agree that
human behavior is contextualized, that human beings
continually put and interpret their own and others
behavior in a context or contexts. Early
interactionists struggled with the idea that in order
to understand the activity of a human being, the social
matrixes or situations in which the activity was
produced must first be determined.

Thomas (1923) suggests that:

> Preliminary to any self determined
> act of behavior there is always a
> stage of examination and deliber-
> ation which we may call the
> definition of the situation
> (1923:42).

Echoing similar concerns, Mead (1934) writes:

> Social psychology. . . presupposes
> an approach to experience from the
> standpoint of the individual, but
> undertakes to determine in
> particular that which belongs to
> this experience because the
> individual. . .belongs to a social
> structure, a social order (1934:1).

For Mead (1934) this social ordering is internalized
through symbolic interaction and experience.

Watzlawick, Beavin and Jackson (1967) also emphasize the importance of studying behavior in context. In the opening pages of their book, The Pragmatics of Human Communication, they describe three "seemingly unrelated" scenarios, whose single common denominator is that each particular scenario "remains unexplainable" until the range of observations are wide enough to include the context in which the phenomena occur (p. 19-21). Watzlawick, et. al., elaborate:

> Failure to realize the intricacies of the relationship between an event and the matrix in which it takes place, between an organism and its environment, either confronts the observer with something "mysterious" or induces him to attribute to his object of study certain properties the object may not possess (1967:21).

Despite the seemingly consensual stand that contexts are important, the most complex issue surrounding this idea---the reciprocal activity of co-creating contexts for the mutual and simultaneous interpretation of behaviors---has largely been ignored. Aside from Bateson (1972), Van Dijk (1972), Watzlawick, Beavin and Jackson (1967), Hall (1976), Cronen and Lannamann (1980), Trueba (1982), and a handful of Symbolic Interactionists (cf. Glasser and Strauss, 1967; McHugh, 1968; Scheff, 1970; Stover, 1974; and Goffman, 1963, 1974) few empirical attempts have been made to delineate the social process of creating contexts---contextualization.

Yet it seems that human beings interact in the face of real and imagined impingements that exist independent of their interaction, but which, do not determine this interaction. These impingements do, however, influence human behavior and human interactivity. Human beings attend to and build off of each other while recognizing the connection between interpersonal and suprapersonal realities. When this recognition of the connection is made explicit and mutual, when what human beings do to, with and for each other is linked to who these human beings are in terms of general social categories, then social processes and representations of context are made to meet at the crux of fluid social life.

Two historically recent events, the Vietnam war, and the continued struggle of feminist women in American society, illuminate context and contextualization. In common with one another, Vietnam veterans and feminist women are trying to create the contexts which they and others use for interpreting their respective experiences and behaviors.

While it has been ten years since the last American soldier was killed in Vietnam (in April 1975, 865 combat marines took part in the evacuation of American personnel from Siagon and on April 28, 1975 Darwin Judge and William McMahon were killed at Tan Son Nhut air base) there have been several attempts to place the war, experiences of the war, American disenchantment with the war, and the returning Vietnam veteran, into a context or contexts. In short, numerous attempts have been made to render this part of contemporary American history understandable. To momentarily focus on one group desperately trying to put the war in context, consider the returned veteran.

Overnight, in relatively small numbers, young men travelled from combat zones in Vietnam to any number of military bases in the United States. With little time in transition they returned to a society which was either disenchanted or disinterested with the war and those who fought it (Markley, 1980).

Many Vietnam veterans feel that the American public has contextualized the Vietnam experience as historical events to be forgotten either because the war "wasn't won" or because it took place at all. There are increasing attempts by veterans to put this experience into a context other than "events to be forgotten." One attempt to introduce a new context was made by artist George L. Skypeck, who wrote beneath his portrait of a Vietnam veteran:

Was the character of my valor less intense than those at Lexington?

Was the pain of my wounds any less severe than those at Normany?

And was my loneliness any less sorrowful than
those at Inchon?

Then why am I forgotten amongst those remembered
as "heroes"??

   The struggle of feminist women in American society,
the second historical issue mentioned, is also a
struggle of context creation. As a group of people in
American society, a group now comprising just a little
over one-half of the total population; women have been
ignored, treated as less than equal to men, studied and
mis-studied. For centuries, persons other than women,
chose the standards to which women would be compared
and by which women's behavior would be judged. Women
and women's behavior were not studied in order to
delineate these standards. Not too surprisingly, women
have been labeled _deficit_ when judged by standards
detached from women's experiences.

   At least two endeavors of feminist women serve as
illustration of this struggle of context creation and
re-creation: 1) research on women's communication and
2) "women's music." First, numerous scholars
interested in women's communication and language use
point out the problems with mis-studying women's
communication (cf. Kramarae, 1980; and Spender, 1981).
As Fine, et al., (1985) explain: "Virtually all of the
research on language and gender treats women as _objects_
of research, an ironic twist to the objectification of
women. Rather than having women explore their own
perceptions of their communication and set their own
priorities for their own communication needs,
researchers have imposed their perceptions and
priorities" (p.2). These imposed perceptions and
priorities have resulted in what Johnson (1982) calls
"the new deficit position," which for our purposes may
be referred to as the new deficit context. From this
perspective, or within this frame: ". . . the
deficiencies in women's language are attributed not to
the nature of women but to the perversions of a sexist
society. Women's language is seen to correspond to
and reinforce the weak social position that women have
in relation to men" (Fine, et al., 1985).

   As a result and as a corrective measure, a
growing number of scholars interested in women's
communication are studying women and women's

30

perceptions in order to create empirically grounded
contexts for understanding the communicative
experiences of women. Increasingly, these scholars are
arguing that a new context is necessary for
understanding and studying what happens when women
talk. In creating this new context, previous studies
are being recontextualized as "mis-studies."

The second phenomenon which illustrates the
struggle of feminist women to create new contexts for
the interpretation and understanding of women's
behavior is "women's music." This type of music,
created by feminist women, "re-presents" the
experiences women have in a world which judges them by
standards developed separate from their own experiences
in that world. Holly Near's song, <u>Lady At The Piano</u>,
illustrates a process of re-contextualizing women's
behavior and experience. As she write/sings:

There's a club down on the avenue
    where the hustlers come to jest
And the lady at the piano who can play
    all their requests
But she grows weary of the standards
    so she sings her own refrain
Until Joe, the noisy bartender, starts in to complain

Lady it seems, you write a pretty melody
but your words are too full of pain
People come to be entertained
They don't want to see you act as they are. . .
    So be a star
Be sparkle, be glitter, be taller, be thinner, be
    sure

One night the club was empty,
    the world series kept them home
So the lady at the piano got to play there all alone
A group came in 'round midnight
    and stayed the whole night long
For the first time someone listened
    to her very special song

Woman it seems, you write a song as if just for me
You spill my life on the floor
Then you shine a light on the door
Don't let them make you weaken and bend. . .
    come sing again

31

Be honest, be giving, remember we're singing
   with you
And the lady said "I do"

But I can't seem to see why now and then
   I go out to see a movie
When the hero is never me so I write
   all this angry poetry
They keep requesting those love songs
They're called "good old fashion love songs"
He and she and a baby make three
I swear they're making crazy people out of me
That club is making crazy people out of me

Well, the lady is still at the piano
   but the clientele has changed
You don't see the noisy hustlers come in after games
The bartender's name is Sophie
   and the bouncer's name is Jane
And the lady, the lady at the piano
Will never be the same

From these examples, one <u>should</u> conclude that
context creation is, indeed, a very serious business.
Not only do Vietnam veterans and Feminist women share
in wanting to create new contexts for interpreting
their own behaviors, and not only do they have in
common the desire to have these new contexts publicly
accepted; but, both these groups of people are
confronting some very structural aspects of context.

Contexts, then, are not things out there, but are
mediated and created by people fitting their lines of
action together. As such it is not simply people like
Joe and Mary who mediate and create contexts, it is
"Vietnam Veteran" Joe and "Feminist" Mary, people with
social identities and pasts. These social identities
and pasts are called out as the more concrete features
of context. The empirical effort of this research is to
delineate the creative process of contextualizing where
contexts emerge from people fitting their lines of
action together. To this end the following section
outlines the known features of context in an attempt to
theoretically define context. This theoretical
definition of context includes a literature review
presented in terms of key focusing concepts. Defining
contexts in this manner provides sensitizing concepts

(Blumer, 1969) necessary to describe contextualization.

Dimensions of Social Context

In Chapter One I suggested that there are six germane elements involved in context and contextualization. As stated these six elements are: social consequences, subjective interpretation, boundaries, shared language and situation, systemic qualities, and refelxivity. While these issues have been introduced in chapter one, each of these aspects or dimensions of context will be elaborated on and discussed separately in this chapter. In so doing, this chapter on the dimensions of context, develops a foundation for chapter three's focus of fanciful recontextualization.

Social Consequences

Existent literature on "the definition of the situation" (cf. Thomas, 1923; and McHugh, 1968) shares many of the same concerns emergent in the "context" literature. Indeed, in discussions of the "definition of the situation" it becomes clear that the term is used synonymous with the term context. It is in the "definition of the situation" literature that the issue of the social consequences of behavior is introduced.

In taking issue with the classical Behaviorists, Thomas and Swaine Thomas (1923) argue that both subjective and objective features of social worlds and contexts and not just objective features be studied in order to adequately understand human actions. As illustration they write:

> . . . the Warden of Donnemore
> prison recently refused to honor
> the order of the court to send an
> inmate outside the prison walls
> for some specific purpose. He
> excused himself on the grounds
> that the man was too dangerous.
> He had killed several persons who
> had the unfortunate habit of
> talking to themselves on the
> street. From the movement of their

33

lips he imagined they were calling
him vile names, and he behaved as
if this were true. If men define
situations as real, they are
real in their consequences" (p.154)
(emphasis mine).

While making the argument that situations defined as
real are real in their consequences, Thomas and Swaine
Thomas (1923) not only introduce the social
consequences of behavior but they also begin the
argument that "subjective interpretation" is necessary
to issues of context.

Subjective Interpretation

When delineating the context of communication,
Cronen and Lannamann (1981) suggest that individual
social actors interpret the meaning of a message
according to particular hierarchical levels of
organized meaning. The hierarchical levels they
identify are: cultural patterns, life scripts,
relationships, episodes, speech acts, and content. Any
one of these levels may provide the context for
interpreting any particular utterance or message.
According to Cronen and Lannamann (1981), since
individuals are interpreters of messages, they are also
the creators of context. Placing or interpreting
meaning in context occurs "in the heads of
individuals." Ultimately, an interacting dyad may
(according to this line of reasoning), be operating
from two very different interpretive contexts. For
instance, one person, because of subjective
interpretation, may be placing the ongoing activity
into the context of "cultural pattern," while the
other may be placing the behavior into the context of
"relationship." Given this hierarchy of meaning which
allows for subjective interpretation, Lannamann (1983)
defines context as "a transparent vantage point around
which a person orients his or her meaning structure"
(p.21).

Keeping with the individual as the unit of
analysis in his discussion of high and low contexts,
Hall (1976), ties context and subjective interpretation
together with culture as the determining factor. Hall
(1976) argues that:

34

One of the functions of culture is to provide a highly selective screen between man and the outside world. This screening function provides structure for the world and protects the nervous system from informational overload. . . . The only way to increase information-handling capacity without increasing the mass and complexity of the system. . .is. . .by means of the contexting process (p.85-86).

The contexting process formulated by Hall (1976) is based on a high---low context continuum. Constituting this context continuum is the degree to which a person is aware of the selective screen they place between themselves and the outside world. Hall (1976) writes: "as one moves from the low to the high side of the scale, awareness of the selective process increases" (p.86). Thus, in high context communication most information is either in the physical context or it is internalized in the person. Very little information is found in the coded, explicit, transmitted part of the message. Low context communication is just the opposite and the "mass of the information is vested in the explicit code" (Hall, 1976:91).

This high-low context continuum serves to introduce the next two aspects of context: boundaries and shared language or coded symbol systems.

Boundaries

While the weight of symbolic interaction theory suggests that defining situations, understanding human behavior in context, and contextualizing are fluid processes in that every human interactive situation is unique; I use the term boundaries to refer to the more structural "taken for granted" aspects of social life that for any number of reasons, are not continually re-negotiated. With the concept of boundaries, the age-old Hobbesian question of : How is social order possible?, is addressed.

35

Gonos (1977) observes that symbolic interactionists consider it their "theoretical calling" to describe the "rich texture of everyday social life" and to that end "they have insisted on study at close range, as participants, and from this vantage point, the situations that make up everyday life have been seen as idiosyncratic" (p.856). And Stebbins's (1967) discussions of the definition of the situation are exemplar of Gonos's (1977) observations. As Stebbins (1967) states:

> Objective situations are unique. In the words of W.I. Thomas, "social situations never spontaneously repeat themselves, every situation is more or less new, for every one includes new human activities differently combined" (p.154).

However, in critically evaluating the notion that everyday social life is idiosyncratic, Goffman (1974) comments that the Thomas's dictum: "If men define situations as real, they are real in their consequences;" is true as it reads, but false as it is taken. As he elaborates: "True, we personally negotiate aspects of all arrangements under which we live, but often once these are negotiated, we continue on mechanically as though the matter had always been settled" (p.2). Goffman (1974) suggests that the fluid interpretation process which Thomas and Swaine Thomas' work introduces, does not adequately address "structural" or micro-structural elements. In other words, the context boundaries have not been adequately dealt with.

Historically, Goffman's work (cf. 1963, 1974) has attempted to deal with the processes of interpersonal relationships from a micro-structural paradigm. In his early work on social occasion Goffman (1963) offers that within time and space constraints there are certain broad rules which regulate interaction. Goffman implies, however, that these rules are loosely formulated since the concept "social occasion" encompasses certain complications. For example, depending upon a person's perspective, what may be an occasion for play for one may be an occasion for work for another. Nevertheless, Goffman insists that participants usually have consensual definitions regarding the social occasions in which they find themselves. Interactants are on the job, at school, shopping, etc.

"Social occasion," as defined by Goffman (1963) is similar to what Lofland (1971) has termed "social setting." According to Lofland, social settings are "forms of human association. . .that provide for those involved in it a similarity of circumstances of action" (1971:16).

Watzlawick, Beavin and Jackson (1967), at one point, describe context as both internally and externally constraining. In other words, social interaction is at once "institutionally" bounded and interactively bounded. They state: "Contexts, then, can be more or less restricting, but always determines the contingencies to some extent" (p.132); moreover, ". . .context does not consist only of institutional, external (to communication) factors. The manifest messages exchanged become part of the particular interpersonal context and place their restrictions on subsequent interaction" (p.132). As they specify: "in a communication sequence, every exchange of messages narrows down the number of possible next moves" (p.131). Context, then, is both internal to a message as well as external to it.

This inside/outside imagery is also offered by Goffman (1974). Goffman (1974) extends his work on social occasions to frame analysis and argues that "boundary markers" are part of framing. These markers are conventional and occur before and after the activity. The boundary markers, according to Goffman (1974):

> . . .like the wooden frame of a
> picture, are presumably neither
> part of the content of the activity
> proper nor part of the world
> outside the activity but rather
> both inside and outside. .
> .(p.252).

As an obvious example, Goffman sites the use of a gavel to both call a meeting to order and then dismiss it.

Bateson (1972), also aware of the structural aspects of context, introduces a notion of psychological frames (p.184-187) as boundaries. These frames limit a set of messages and/or meaningful actions. As with Goffman (1974) and Watzlawick, Beavin and Jackson (1967), Bateson's (1972) psychological frames are both exclusive and inclusive: "by excluding certain meaningful actions (certain others) are included" (p.187). Further, psychological frames are related to "premises;" messages and meaningful actions are part of a universe of relevance that persons share with one another.

"How" boundaries emerge and stabilize, and how these become social, are important questions to address. To this end Malinowski (1923), Whorf (1958), and Mead (1934) attribute the emergence of boundaries to the use of shared language.

Shared Language

Boundaries as structural elements of context are possible when shared meaning parameters exist. And shared meanings are possible only with a shared symbol system. Symbol use allows us to name our worlds into existence and to thereby act on the named world.

In his early fieldwork, Malinowski, confronts the notion of "context of situation," and here he suggests that context and meaning are dependent. Specifically, Malinowski argues that language as action should be the focus for students of human behavior interested in linguistics. The analysis of common or shared language use, he argues provides the opportunity to study meaning creation.

Mead (1934) also associates meaning creation with language or significant symbol use. Langauge is shared and, by nature, its use is communication.

In explaining Mead's work, Miller (1973) writes:

> Language, gestures, significant
> symbols, have common or shared
> meanings in the sense that they
> evoke functionally identical
> responses in the various members of

the group who use and understand
those gestures. The response
elicited by a word or sentence
that is understood is, first of
all, an inhibited response or a
covert or implicit response, or
delayed overt response. It is the
beginning of an overt response, and
it controls the later phases of the
social act.

By controlling responses and thus the later phases of
the social act, shared language becomes a necessary
condition for context creation.

Similarly, Whorf (1956) illustrates how the name
given a situation affects a person's behavior in that
situation. He notes:

. . .around a storage of what are
called gasoline drums, behavior
will tend to a certain type, that
is great care will be exercise;
while around a storage of what are
called empty gasoline drums, it
will tend to be different---care-
less, with little repression of
smoking or of tossing cigarette
butts about" (p.160-161).

Whorf asserts that the latter, empty gasoline drums,
are more dangerous than the former since they contain
"explosive vapor." Linguistic analysis, somewhat
paradoxically, reveals that the word empty suggests
that there is a lack of hazard. Lack of hazard, then,
becomes the definition of the situation and gives rise
to particular behavioral patterns---in this case
carelessness.

It is by and through language that information is
shared and transmitted. Many argue (cf. Bateson, 1972;
Watzlawick, Beavin and Jackson, 1967; and Millar, 1980)
that as information is created and transmitted by and
through language, it is also transmitted by and through
a cybernetic or systemic process.

Systemic Qualities

Cybernetics deals with the transmission of information (communication) within and among systems and their environments and attempts to assess the effect which this information input and output has in patterning the systems behavior. A central and defining feature of cybernetics is its concern with the extent to which information input, via feedback mechanisms, allows a system to be self-regulating (correcting, directing, and purposive), in terms of its behavior, vis-a-vis its environment. This environment might include other systems.

Cybernetics, hence, focuses on the manner in which open systems organize and constrain their behavior in regard to the information obtained from their relevant environments. The mode of analysis employed in cybernetics is what Bateson (1972) calls "negative explanation." The key differentiating features of the method are as follows:

> Causal explanation is usually positive. We usually say the billiard ball B moved in such and such a direction because billiard ball A hit it at such and such an angle. In contrast to this cybernetic explanation is always negative. We consider what alternative possibilities could have occured and then ask why many of the alternatives were not followed, so that the particular event was one of the few which could, in fact, occur (Bateson, 1972:399).

Negative explanation is comparable to the logical form known as reductio ad absurdum, where a set of mutually exclusive propositions are enumerated and all but one is eliminated as untenable. Moreover, whereas positive explanation usually proceeds by some form of analysis in which the whole is explained in terms of (by reduction to) its constitutive parts; cybernetics employs the antithetical strategy where the part is made explicable by placing it in the context of an overarching whole. As Bateson (1972) writes:

This hierarchy of contexts within contexts is universal for the communicational (or emic) aspect of phenomena and drives the scientist always to seek for explanation in the ever larger units. It may (perhaps) be true in physics that the explanation of the macroscopic is to be sought in the microscopic. The opposite is usually true in cybernetics: without contexts there is not communication (p.402).

Astutely, Stover (1974) points out the ontological similarities between cybernetic theory and symbolic interaction theory. Stover (1974) argues that Mead's (1934) notion of a social act is a definition of context, but that it in and of itself, lacks the hierarchical conceptualization which makes the Palo Alto vision theoretically rich. He suggests that a merger between cybernetics and symbolic interaction would allow for specifying "pyramiding contexts within which the social act occurs" (p.11). Stover's (1974) version of this pyramid includes roles interactants enact, institutional and organizational settings, and, symbols employed in the act.

Stover (1974) points out that his incorporation of hierarchy and informational systems into a symbolic interactionist theory of social context gets beyond Glasser and Strauss's (1967) hallmark account of social context as awareness contexts. While it is true that Glasser and Strauss (1967) do not incorporate a hierarchical conceptualization into their account of social contexts, they do have an information bias.

To momentarily backtrack, Glasser and Strauss (1967) introduce the concept of awareness context to facilitate the understanding of human interaction. Accordingly, they define awareness context as:

. . .the total combination of what each interactant in a situation knows about the identity of the other and his own identity in the eyes of the other (p.337).

41

Conceptually, awareness contexts are structural units ". . .of an encompassing order larger than the other units under focus: interaction. Thus an awareness context surrounds and affects the interaction" (Glasser and Strauss, 1967:337).

Reflexivity is conceptually related to context when one adopts a hierarchical view of communication, as suggested by the Palo Alto group. Two other notions of reflexivity, one forwarded by Cronen and Lannamann (1981) and Burke (1945) are relevant here.

Reflexivity

Cronen and Lannamann (1980) suggest that reflexivity is ubiquitous and as such is essential to human communication. As presented in the first chapter, Cronen and Lannamann (1980) argue that: "reflexivity exists whenever two elements in a hierarchical system are organized so that each is simultaneously context for and contexted by the other" (p.1). In recall, they present a hierarchy of meaning encompassing the levels of: content, speech acts, episode, relationship, life script, and cultural patterns. Their notion of reflexivity suggests that any level, of the hierarchy of meaning can be either context for or contexted by any other level. There is no static ordering to the hierarchy and its manifestations.

Burke (1945) deals with the container and the thing contained by introducing ratios. Each ratio forms a dual leveled hierarchy where a reflexive relationship emerges between the two levels. At times "scenes contain acts," or "scenes contain agents." Interestingly, Burke (1945) insists that of the ratios he identifies (ten in all) "both act and agent require scenes that "contain" them" (p.15). While positing a flexible, hierarchical, and reflexive theory of human interaction (or symbolic action) Burke (1945), like Goffman (1963, 1974), recognizes that there are some "structure-like," non re-negotiable elements to social life. (While I agree that there are non re-negotiable elements to social life, as will become apparent, Burke's scene as container of acts and agents is not necessarily one of them. I use Burke's pentad and ratios as heuristic devices which allow for a particular kind of analysis of social life.

42

Specifically, Burke's ratios are used in my analysis to allow for a discussion of reflexivity).

To illustrate one of these ratios, the scene-act ratio, Burke (1945) writes:

> Among the most succinct instances of the scene-act ratio in dialetical materialism is Marx's assertion. . .that "Justice can never rise superior to the economic conditions of society and the cultural development conditioned by them." That is, in contrast with those who would place justice as a property of personality (an attribute purely of agent), the dialectical materialist would place it as a property of the material situation (economic conditions), the scene in which justice is to be enacted. He would say that no higher quality of justice can be enacted than the nature of the scenic properties permits (p.13).

Summary

Context, I argue, is a very serious and complex issue. Much has been written about context, not enough empirically grounded research has been conducted on the process of contextualization. That task is the one at hand. Two very important considerations accompany the study of context and context creation: first, the six elements abstracted from the existing literature on context must be addressed; second, contextualization must be tied to some empirically observable behavior. I take both of these concerns into account.

Regarding the first concern, the data generated for this study remain true to the six identified aspects of context by incorporating them as observable. As such the consequences of social action are captured on video tape as live interaction constitutes the data base. Subjective interpretation, as Mead (1934) suggests, is observed as "responsiveness" and "responses." The data generated is bounded by a serious

43

ongoing task which is facilitated by language. Since language use or talk is part of the data, information transmitted and information transmission are rendered observable. Finally, the systemic qualities of cybernetic modelling and a Burkean conceptualization of reflexivity are <u>analytically</u> incorporated into this research project.

As for the second concern: observable behavior for studying context creation, the next chapter should be informative. Contextualization is studied here as fanciful recontextualization.

C H A P T E R   T H R E E

HIERARCHICAL MODEL OF FANCIFUL

RECONTEXTUALIZATION

> (H)uman play finds its true
> perfection in being art, the
> 'transformation into structure.'
> Only through its development does
> play acquire its ideality, so that
> it can be intended and understood
> as play. Only now does it emerge
> as detached from the presenting
> activity of the players and consist
> in the pure appearance of what they
> are playing. As such the
> play---even the unforseen elements
> of improvisation---is fundamentally
> repeatable and hence permanent. It
> has the character of a work of an
> ergon and not only energia. In
> this sense I call it a structure.
> (Gadamer, 1982)

Defining Play

In agreement with Simmel, Duncan (1962) wrote:
"the purest form of relationship among equals exists in
social play," (1962:328), and that "the social spirit
of play comes to full expression in the deep sense of
solidarity we experience when we play together."
Further, Simmel (1950) and Duncan (1962) attempt to
conceptualize human play as communicative phenomena
which involves the process of recontextualization.
Others, most notably Bateson (1972) [1], Goffman
(1974) and Bolough (1976) have attempted a similar
conceptualization of play.

Play, in this work, is viewed from a symbolic
interaction standpoint of social behavior as
continually being constructed by people functioning in
a cooperative fashion [2]. Facilitating and making
possible this cooperation is language and language
use. On this point Mead and Burke are informative.
In Mead's (1934) terms the ability of humans to

45

produce cooperative action is based on conversations of significant symbols where symbols which are significant: "arouse in the other individual the same idea it arouses in the first" (p.46).

The focus for studying play is on how people coordinate their respective behaviors to construct concerted units. People as independently acting units create social contexts within which their independent behaviors are defined. These contexts, once constructed, are not static but are reflexive and impinge on the creators, who in turn reconstruct or recontextualize the "context" and thus the meaning of the reciprocal behavior.

With recontextualization thematically integral to the understanding of play, context and contextualizing are reintroduced. In formulating a definition of play as communicative behavior, one other theme emerges as an integrally related concept: metacommunication. This is introduced in Bateson's (1972) work on play. With metacommunication serving as a conceptual foundation play may be defined as a transformational social act.

Metacommunication and Play:
Transformational Social Act

In general, metacommunication is anything that "contextualizes" or frames messages. Although, Bateson (1972) is concerned largely with metacommunication in animals, in particular as metacommunication is involved in the communication of play signals, a number of behavioral scientists have picked up on the concept and have attempted to refine it. Refinement of this concept is of absolute necessity to social scientists who not only find it an intriguing concept but who want to use it in the construction of communication theory.

In arguing the importance of the refinement of the concept of metacommunication, Altman (1962) observes that: ". . . there has been no formal theory of the basic nature of metacommunication in sufficient operational terms. . . to know just when you had a example of it" (p. 356-357) Echoing similar concerns Bochner and Krueger (1979) offer that: "although the ideas of control, metacommunication, and context are commonly, even axiomatically, assumed to be important, the literature on interpersonal communication shows them to be muddled, inoperable or vague" (p.197).

As the criticisms of metacommunication suggest many competing, although not exhaustive, definitions of the concept exist. For instance, Thorpe (1972) claims that metacommunication only occurs in human interaction, in particular human speech. McBride (1968) along these same lines implicates metacommunication in the evolution of human language, while Sheflen (1974) argues that metacommunicative behaviors are essential in both verbal and non-verbal human interactions. According to Hinde (1972) metacommunication is reflexivness, or the ability to communicate about a system itself. Norton (1978) equates communicator style with metacommunication as it signals to the other (verbally and paraverbally) how to interpret the transaction. While Wilmot (1980) writes that metacommunication occurs "whenever one person comments on... ongoing communicative transactions. . ." (p.64). He goes on to argue that most of the confusion surrounding this concept would be cleared up once relational and episodic levels of communication have been distinguished.

Millar (1980) also in hopes of de-muddling the concept claims that the importance of the term 'metacommunication' lies in the "shaking of our accepted epistemology" (p.2). In illustrating this epistemological shake-up Millar (1980) draws out the connections between metacommunication and language. In grappling with these connections, Millar (1980) writes: ". . . in any formalized language. . . in order to assert that any given statement is true or not; one must first establish a conceptual context." Accordingly, in order to evaluate 'truth' statements one must develop/accept certain values/assumptions about the world. Language must be internalized for this to occur. Once internalized, language guides perceptions. As Castaneda (1974) explains: "The world we perceive . . . is an illusion. It was created by a description that was told us since the moment we were born" (p.101).

While there are many disputes surrounding the term metacommunication, there does seem to exist an underlying logic. Specifically, metacommunication

refers---regardless of the content of the behavior
observed---to a process of transcending levels of
meaning and interpretation of behavior.

Beckoff (1975) in applying the underlying logic
of metacommunication to a concern with the function
of play signals offers that ". . . metacommunication
will have occured when it can be shown that the
performance of a particular behavior(s) has served to
alter the significance of a subsequent signal(s)" (p.
232). Beckoff's (1975) conceptualization allows for
the development of the perspective on play as
transformational social act. This notion of play is
consistent with the conceptualization of Simmel
(1950). The idea of play as transformational social
act deserves elaboration.

Play as a social act [3] involves the fanciful
recontextaulization of ongoing social interaction.
interacting implies communicating and it is through
communication that individuals coordinate their
activities (Mead,1934). As mentioned in the first
chapter, while relating play to communication Simmel
(1950), distinguished between form and content in human
communication. For him the play form emerges from the
contents of ordinary or serious life situations, but
ultimately is not bound in these.

> Play like art, developed originally
> out of the realities of life, yet
> both have created spheres which
> preserve their autonomy in face of
> these realities. This autonomy, in
> play as in art, still draws its
> strength from its origin in life,
> which keeps them permeated with
> life. . . . Yet it is not until the
> forms of play and art are
> separated from the purposes and
> needs of the community and become
> the purposes and means of their own
> existence as forms that they
> become true play and art. From
> the realities of life (art and
> play) take only what they can adapt
> to their own nature, only what
> they can absorb in their autonomous
> existence (Simmel, 1950:4243).

48

Simmel (1950) also offers coquetry (p.50-51) as exemplar of play and playfulness. As Bolough (1976) in explaining Simmel's example states: "Here the content is eroticism. We may treat coquetry as abstracting out the form---how eroticism is accomplished with the emphasis on the how---and expressing behaviorally, but without the content or purpose what is ordinarily associated with eroticism---mating" (p.114). Simmel's (1950) observations are consistent with Huizinga's (1960) description of institutional play in which he considers play as a flight from ordinary reality. Miller (1973) also discusses the beneficial consequences that emerge from play which are independent of their original content of the particular context. Simmel's (1950) thematic connection of play and art is reflected in the works of others. For instance, Gadamer (1975) uses the concept of play to provide clues to the ontology of art. He too argues that the similarity of play and art lies in the form of abstraction from the mundane or 'real.' Moreover, he joins with others (c.f. Bateson, 1972; Simmel, 1950; Bolough, 1976) in pointing out the transformational nature of human play (p.99). Glasser (1982), in the spirit of Stephenson's play theory of mass communication (1967) ties newsreading to both Mead's notion of an aesthetic experience and play. More specifically, Glasser argues that "newsreading as play---the pleasurable but disinterested state that an individual creates and fashions when reading a newspaper---transcends the utility or usefulness of the newspaper" (p.101).

Combs (1982) sees play as a useful concept in the study of popular culture. He claims that "the concept of play permits us to better understand the 'linkage' between popular communication and 'serious' worlds such as politics" (p.5). In illustrating this he offers that the 'play' of drama allows for 'play-fantasies' which may be enacted in 'serious' real-life contexts. As he insists:

> I suspect that both elite and mass
> fantasies have been fed by the
> heroic ' depictions of such
> successful daring raids as the
> Israeli raid at Entebbe. That such
> commando raids are risky seems
> subdued by the dramatic glory of

pulling it off just like in the
popular account. The play stirs
play-fantasies about repeating the
play in another 'real-life'
context, that somehow the play of
political life can and should
live up to the dramatic standards
of art" (p.7).

Bolough (1976) points out that Simmel's (1950) notion
of form and content is analogous to Bateson's (1972)
idea of metacommunication. In recall, to Bateson
(1972) metacommunication involves the recognition of
signs as signals which are only signals.
Metacommunication, as Bateson defines it, refers to
the denotative messages among animals and human beings
who engage in interaction sequences. When play occurs
the seriousness or literalness of messages are
transformed and not meant as they might be ordinarily.

Bolough (1976) elaborates on this notion of
transcendence and adds yet another term to describing
it. What Bateson (1972) calls metacommunication and
Simmel (1950) calls form, Bolough (1976) calls
abstracting. Her concept of abstracting goes one step
further than Simmel and Bateson. Bolough (1976), in
delineating the concept and process of abstracting,
argues that the abstracting nature of play is actually
the transforming of a deep rule which is one among the
four which make serious social action possible.

Relevant to metacommunication is Goffman's (1974)
concept of keying. When keying occur, previously
agreed upon meaning that allows people to interact is
transformed. The meaning conveyed, then, is newly
emergent or implicit, yet still dependent upon what
was previously established or explicit. The primary
framework provides the interactants with something not
literal or actually occuring (implicit). In this
manner, playing---play for play's sake---is
distinguished from the activity from which it emerged.
Goffman (1974) ties keys and keying to his concept of
frame. As already discussed, frames are analogous to
context.

Simmel (1950), Bateson (1972), Bolough (1976) and
Goffman (1974) all suggest that the concept of play
implies ". . . an ability to differentiate play from

the 'real' and the 'serious' " (Kochman, 1981: 52).
Kochman (1981) makes this same observation regarding
"verbal play" as in signifying or playing the dozens.
Abrahams (1976), along these same lines, suggests that
for play to function effectively as play (the play for
play's sake phenomenon) "there must be a sense of
threat arising from the real and serious world of
behavior" (p.40).

"Galumping" is a term coined by Miller (1973) to
describe a complex form of play exhibited by babboons
which he also applies to human playful activity.
Based on observations, Miller (1973) concludes that in
play the process of attaining goals becomes more
important than the goals themselves. He defines
"galumping" as: "patterned, voluntary elaboration or
complication of process, where the pattern is not
under the dominant control of goals" (p.92). It
provides a frame or context for novel behavior free
from the control of previously set limits. As he
writes: "Play is a context, or . . . frame. It is a
mode of organization of behavior---a way of fitting
pieces of activity together" (Miller, 1973:92). This
is similar to Goffman's keying and Bateson's
metacommunication in playful interaction.

Lastly, Miller (1973) and Bolough (1976) suggest
that play allows for individual autonomy. Miller
(1973) introduces autonomy when he writes: "Play
involves a relative autonomy of means. Ends are not
obliterated, but they don't. . . determine the means. .
. . This state of affairs implies a degree of autonomy
for the actor. . . which makes for freedom to assume
roles otherwise unreal" (p.92). Bolough (1976) argues
that: "playfulness is a display of detachment which
is the basis of individual freedom" (p.119).

Fanciful recontextualization is a flight into
fantasy which recontextualizes or transforms the
consequences of interaction. The activity is denoted
metacommunicatively as the participants differentiate
between the explicit literal content and the implicit
process of whimsical fantasy. One note of caution:
although it is argued that play transforms
consequences, I am not arguing that there are not
consequences to play. Play as Huizinga (1955) points
out, can be very serious business.

51

Fanciful Recontextualization
Hierarchically Arranged

There are three hierarchical levels of analysis within which human play may be studied. Each following level is dependent upon the previous. First, is individual play; second social play; and third, public play. While the first and third levels will be discussed, the research focuses, for the most part, on the second hierarchical level---social play. What is different about or what distinguishes each of these levels from one another are the consequences of the activity. The distinctions identifiable between each level of play are heuristic distinctions. Consequently the hierarchical model of play is simply an organizational procedure developed from both the current literature on play as well as observations made regarding the activity. The distinctions noted between each level of play are theoretical allowing for further discovery and exploration of the topic of play and context creation.

Briefly, individual play is largely a cognitive activity where individuals fancifully imagine overt activity. Contrastly, social play has the social function of creating solidarity among equals. Further, while engaging in social play the participants can make comments upon their relationship with one another. The consequences of this type of play are the creation of cohesion and reifying social relationships. Lastly, public play, not only has the potential consequence of making comments on existing social relationships with the intention of altering them; but this third type of play has the potential of, at least temporarily, altering authoritative relationships. Public play is purposeful and is persuasive.

All human action is situationally bound, it is within social situations (or Goffman's, 1963, social occasion) that contexts are created. Contextualization is possible as persons create social worlds through discourse. Within a single social situation or frame multiple contexts may emerge over time. For instance, during the course of a cocktail party social actors may form and transform a series of contexts which may be defined (labelled) as playful, serious, ritual, work, etc.

For contexts within situational boundaries to emerge social actors must share a language, they must be able to transmit and receive information (in the sense of Turner's, 1962, role-taking). Humans must also be reflexive about their's and other's behavior. This reflexivity is only possible through processes of subjective interpretation.

Individual Play

Individual play is possible only when one has a rudimentary symbol system; more specifically, when one is able to attend to one's self as an object. Moreover, individual play is only possible when one is able to project a future. As an example of individual play consider the following scenario: In a required graduate-level theory class the students encounter a rather pompous and arrogant professor who frequently makes the comment that: "His peers are either dead or yet unborn." To ease the pain and make light of the situation, a student in the class may simply tell herself: "Whomever his peers, he still has a penis and looks silly naked."

Social Play

Social play accentuates social situations and social relationships. As example, the following episode of interaction occured between a father, his teenaged son, and a friend of the son when the three were walking home from a bus stop. The father noticed that the sun appeared to be streaming from the sky.

> father: When I was a kid they used to tell us that the sun streams were angles dancing down from heaven. Can you believe the shit they'd tell kids then?

> son: Dad, you're not suppose to say things like that!!!

> father: Oh, well, son, did you know that those sun streams are angles dancing down from heaven?

53

son: (as   an   aside to his friend)
Can you   believe   the   shit they'll
tell kids?

(all three laugh)

In   accentuating   the   unequal   social   relationship
while engaging in   social   play,   two   things occur.
First,   the   participants   engage   in   distancing
themselves from their social roles in   order to comment
on them.   In   this   example of social play both the
father and the son   do this.   Second,   while creating
this   role   distance   and subsequently, by 'poking fun'
at   the   social   roles   the   participants paradoxically
reinforce their   social roles.

Public Play

Public play,   the third and last type of play, has
as   constitutive   elements   purposefulness   and
persuasion.   Regarding these two   constitutive elements
some of Burke's work   is   noteworthy.   According   to
Burke (1969)   persuasion is the ancestral for rhetoric.
Rhetoric   is   public   communication.   In associating
rhetoric and persuasion Burke   (1969) writes: "Whenever
there   is   persuasion there   is rhetoric.   And   whenever
there   is meaning there   is persuasion."

In   elaborating   persuasion   as the ancestral term
of   rhetoric,   Burke,   adds   the   notion   of
"identification."   Identification   becomes Burke's key
term for rhetoric (Nichols,   1971:100).   According   to
Burke, one   persuades by   "identifying" one's ways with
those of the   audience.   Burke is clear   in the position
that identification or   identifying and being identical
are not   one   and   the   same.   Here   his   notion of
"consubstantiality" is important.

A   is   not   identical   with   his
colleague, B. But insofar   as their
interests   are   joined,   A   is
identified   with B.   Or   he   may
identify   himself   with   B   even
when   their   interests   are   not
joined,   if   he   assumes   that they
are,   or   is   persuaded   to believe
so. . . . In   being   identified   with

54

> B, A is "substantially" with a
> person other than himself. Yet
> at the same time he remains
> unique. . . . Thus he is both
> joined and separate, at once a
> distinct substance and
> consubstantial with another"
> (Burke, 1969: 20-21).

A paradox is manifest at the crux of the terms
identification and consubstantiality (as all Burke's
terms seem paradoxical). Simultaneously persons are
identified with and unique from that which they are
identified, and moreover with whom they and what they
understand.

> A doctrine of consubstantiality,
> either implicitly or explicitly
> may be necessary to any way of
> life. For substance, in the old
> philosophies, was an act; and a way
> of life is an acting together; and
> in acting together, men have common
> sensations, concepts, images,
> ideas, attitudes, that make them
> consubstantial (Burke, 1969: 21).

Language allows for persuasion, identification and
consubstantiality: "You persuade a man only in so far
as you can talk his langauge by speech, gesture,
tonality, order, image, attitude, idea, identifying
your way with his" (Burke, 1969). Furthermore, Burke
writes that language is "most public, most collective
in its substance." Language use provides the means by
which people are able to identify and thereby persuade
one another: ". . . identification is hardly other
than a name for the function of sociality" (Duncan,
1962:159). The claim becomes, then, that for
persuasion, identification, or consubstantiality to
emerge, reciprocal activity between people must take
place---social interaction facilitated by language is
necessary.

One Flew Over The Cuckoo's Nest

Ken Kesey's portrayal (as filmically interpreted
by Milos Forman) of a group encounter session that is

transformed into an imaginary baseball game announced by Patric McMurphy in One Flew Over the Cuckoo's Nest, is an example of this process of public play. Moreover, this example is illustrative of how fanciful recontextualization takes place within the institutional and situational boundaries of an authoritarian relationship. Because of the nature of the institutional setting and the type of relationship portrayed, the activity of playing becomes a powerful means of public communication which momentarily renders the tyrannical nature of the relationship void.

Before continuing with this example let me draw attention to the very important "type of relationship" distinction between this hierarchical level of play and the previous one. In the example used to describe social play the relationship between the father and son may, at a formal level, be described as paternalistically authoritarian. In contrast, the relationship between nurse Ratchett and her patients may, at a formal level be described as tyrannically authoritarian. This difference in authoritarian relationships makes all the difference.

Miller, Wielland and Couch (1978) argue that there are many formal types of authority. In differentiating paternalistic authority from tyrannical authority they suggest that the first type has egalitarianism as its ultimate goal. In other words, persons engage in paternalistic authority with the intention. that at some time in the future the participants will be equals. This is not the case with tyrannical authority. Persons participating in this type of authority understand that the superordinate/subordinate relationship is a permanent state. There is no intention of power change short of revolution.

In the institutional setting of a nuthouse McMurphy and the other patients who can function are together with nurse Ratchett in a group therapy session, a routine feature in the insane asylum. During the course of this session, McMurphy introduces the topic of the World Series and reminds nurse Ratchett that it is on television. He further suggests that all involved conclude the session so that he and the other patients can view the game. Nurse Ratchett (affectionately called Big Nurse) informs McMurphy that his suggestion is inappropriate in that it is not only disruptive in relation to the group therapy session, but it is against the rules to watch television in the afternoon. An extended negotiation between McMurphy and nurse Ratchett emerges and finally "Big Nurse" suggests that a vote be taken in the interest of democracy. This is advantageous to her as many of the other patients do not want to publicly challenge her authority. The vote is close, but nurse Ratchett prevails. Television is denied and McMurphy's challenge is apparently rebuffed.

McMurphy's attempt to elicit social support vis-a-vis his direct conflict with Ratchett may have failed, but he does receive social support regarding another focus. This indirectly, but as it turns out, more powerfully challenges Ratchett's authority. After the vote, the undaunted McMurphy gathers the patients around the television set and "announces" a game with the affect of a partisan broadcaster. One by one the patients become highly responsive, even the ones who were considered hopelessly unresponsive or catatonic, and before long the ward is filled with frenzied laughter and cheering.

This cheering is disruptive to the norm of silence that Ratchett insisted upon, but as an onlooker---as the newly created audience---she is forced into the untenable position she had tried to create for McMurphy. The emergent disruption of the routine is non-therapeutic and disorderly, but if she exercises her authority and tells them to stop, she is, in effect, acknowledging that McMurphy's challenge to her authority was successful. If she does not acknowledge McMurphy's challenge--her authority is also challenged because of their unwarranted disruption.

It is clear that McMurphy is able to identify (in Burkean terms) his position as well as nurse Ratchett's and to act in such a way as to comment on the position or standpoints. In making this comment he is purposefully acting in such a way as to persuade her to alter her position. Both McMurphy's position and Rachett's position, ideationally, are tied to some grim contingencies of social life---that not all persons are allowed to act with equal impact on the world: that there are power differentials.

The act named in this episode is the fanciful recontextualization of the ongoing serious context of doing the relationship of an insane asylum. Lurking in the background of this act, the scene, is the tyrannical authoritarian relationship of Big Nurse and the inmates of the asylum. An outcome of this authoritarian relationship as scene is that the persons or agents performing the act or recontextualization are relationally superordinate and subordinate. Discourse and imagination (the ability to project a future) are the agency or instruments used. Moreover, facilitating the completion of this act of fanciful recontextualization is the ability to accurately identify the differing positions of the superordinate and subordinate. The ability to successfully role-take (Mead, 1934; Turner, 1962) is also encompassed as agency. Persuasion, the attempt to comment on the authoritarian relationship between the nurse and her patients, as well as to temporarily alter it, become the purpose.

Nurse Ratchett, by virtue of her untenable position, finds herself in a double-bind [4] context as a consequence of the playful activity contextualized by McMurphy and the other patients. To locate the contextualized acts which frame this double-bind context, allows me to speak of contexts within contexts that are framed at various levels of abstraction. By contextualizing their behavior as play, ie. creating an imaginary baseball game, the patients invite a double-bind context for nurse Ratchett that fits into and overlaps with other contexts that recontextualize the ongoing reality. Briefly, these contexts within contexts can be seen as the interplay or intertwining of act and scene, where, from different standpoints, one contextualizes the other in a hierarchical fashion (eg. at one point act contextualizes scene, and at the other the reverse is the case).

In a broad sense, the patients and nurse Ratchett are together in an institutional situation which contains various constraints and rules of behavior. Within this institutional situation is the practice of therapy, or a therapeutic context. Within the contexts of institutional therapy are the specific personal problems that the patients are required to discuss within the situation of a group session. Further, encompassed within these contexts are the identities that are accentuated within another context involving the mode of interaction that reflects the strategic tension (see Goffman, 1958) of total institutions. Through interaction of this type, categorical, functional, and personal identities intertwine and subsequently are differentially focused on. What often emerges are secondary adjustments (Goffman, 1958:34) made by patients which discreetly challenge staff's authority. In this example, however, the conflictual relationship constructed by McMurphy and Ratchett emerge within these contexts. This dyadic tension is eventually extended to involve the other patients who become instrumental (they are important in that they have a vote) when another context emerges, the vote. Finally, in relation to and contained within these contexts, McMurphy and the patients recontextualize their ongoing present by enacting an imaginary baseball game.

In analyzing this episode in relation to act and scene, it becomes apparent that the two are inseparable and that aspects of one reflect on the aspects of the other. Play or fanciful recontextualization becomes a powerful act of public communication in relation to the scene of "authoritarian relationship," since each of these challenges the other and transforms the consequences of the other. Play, the act, renders the authoritarian relationship temporarily egalitarian. Nurse Ratchett, the authority, is put in the same position (a double-bind) that McMurphy and the other patients are daily placed. The scene of authoritarian relationship transforms or gives multiple meaning to the activity of play. First, the act of play is an act of solidarity (Duncan, 1962) between the patients in the nuthouse. But the act of playing becomes even more important as a challenge to the scene of authority. Playing threatens the disintegration of authority.

In situations where act challenges scene, specifically where playing challenges authority, public play occurs or emerges. This type of play or fanciful recontextualization is significantly different from the two other types of play discussed. It is

possible, however,   only if persons are able to engage
in the two other types of play---individual and social.

Summary

   Play is defined as fanciful recontextualization.
This   definition   makes   metacommunication   and
contextualization   integral to an   understanding of
human social play. With play defined as the process
or more specifically a process of recontextualization,
a hierarchical   model of types of play can be
formulated.   I have done so in this   chapter.
Individual play, social play, and public play
constitute a hierarchical formulation of human play.
The theory of context creation developed in this book
will focus on instances of social play.

Endnotes

1. Although I cite Bateson's work as appearing in the year 1972 it was actually first published in 1955. I am merely relying on the text of the article which was reprinted in 1972.

2. In this work I am using the terms cooperation and coordination as one and the same. I believe I am following Mead's (1934) lead on this. I do recognize that in recent years some communication theorists have made the distinction between coordination and cooperation and coorientation (see, Preace and Cronen, 1981).

3. Mead (1934) defines a social act in the following way:

> The social act is not explained by building it up out of stimulus plus response; it must be taken as a dynamic whole---as something going on---no part of which can be considered or understood by itself---a complete organic process implied by each individual stimulus and response to it (p.7).

4. Double-bind is a communication term introduced by Bateson (1956). This concept refers to a situation where there are: two or more persons, one of whom is a victim; repeated experiences, of; a primary negative injuction; a secondary injunction conflicting with the first only at a more abstract level where the injunction is enforced by punishment or signals which threaten survival; and a tertiary negative injunction prohibiting the victim from escaping from the field.

61

C H A P T E R   F O U R

METHODOLOGY AND METHOD

(R)esearchers should choose their
methods to deal with the concrete
problems they face in any particular research setting rather than to
satisfy some preconceived biases
about methods. (Douglas, 1976: 12).

Introduction

As chapter one indicates the approach taken in this
research is the generation of grounded theory.
Observation, induction, and deduction, the three
pillars of science---are incorporated into this
approach. It is at different parts of the research
endeavor that each of these is incorporated. Based on
observation, theory is grounded or induced (and not
tested). Deduction enters into the research act at two
separate points: first, at the beginning of the
research when decisions regarding data generation are
made; second, when induced theory is discussed in terms
of what is "known." For two reasons a more deductive
method of theory and hypothesis testing is
inappropriate for completing this study. First,
there exists no comprehensive theory of context
creation or contextualization from a communication
perspective. Second, no systematic body of knowledge
of the interpersonal construction of contexts has been
formulated in the social sciences. At best there are
disjointed hypotheses, many of which are not grounded.
This paucity of grounded theory and communication
conceptualizations demands the development and
implementation of research strategies, tools, and
techniques which allows for the generation, recording
and analysis of data pertinent to the research problem.

All social scientists are faced with the task of
generating data which can be systematically analyzed.
I employ the methods of participant observation,
ethnography, and the videotaping of naturally occuring
social interaction. Such data generation techniques
enable me to meet three salient criteria for the study

of concerted behavior, from an interactionist
perspective. First, a focus on naturally occuring
social activity provides the opportunity to view
interaction in which people concert their behaviors;
second, ethnographic techniques satisfy the criteria of
viewing joint behavior within known parameters which
impinge upon interactants and informs them of the
consequences of their activity; and third, the
naturalistic inquiry technique of participant
observation ensures that interactants are allowed to
formulate their own plans of action.

Data Generation Techniques

The central strategy of my research is to collect
and analyze data in such a way as to change the nature
and integrity of the natural world as little as
possible.

While each of the techniques I use have advantages
as singular or individual techniques, they become more
powerful as they are combined. In many ways video and
audio recordings are the "cadillac" of data generation
tools for social scientists.

Video Recordings

The social scientist seeks to
explain human activity. The
accomplishment of this task
requires that researchers make
systematic observations of ongoing
human activity, yet at the same
time achieve sufficient detachment
from the data to detect the order
of the social activity. The task
is to observe interpersonal
events in order to detect how they
fit together in patterns of joint
activities commonly called social
structures and then to accurately
describe to others the order
detected. The ultimate goal is to
accurately describe and explain how
joint activities are created,
sustained, and changed. Recordings
allow researchers to capture and

64

preserve social activities in a
manner no other technology
approaches. Recordings might be to
social scientists what the
microscope is to biologists and
the telescope to astronomers.
(Saxton and Couch, 1975:255)

Capturing sequences of events on videotape allows
for searching and re-searching through the sequenced
events in a manner not possible when limited to direct
and unaided observation. Moreover, video recordings
enable researchers to construct transcripts of the
interaction. With transcripts as concrete accounts of
the interaction being investigated, the researchers
"search" is aided. For all of the instances of
fanciful recontextualization being analyzed,
transcriptions have been made (consult Appendix A for
inclusive transcripts of fanciful recontextualization).
Each transcript contains detailed descriptions of the
interaction being analyzed. Both verbal and nonverbal
gestures are depicted in the transcripts. Further, the
social timing of the conversations are concretely
represented as well as any interruptions in the
discourse. Figure A illustrates social action as
it is transcribed (see next page).

This is a particular episode from the data being
analyzed in this research. What transpires is, first,
confusion over what a specific questionnaire item
response is and then, play, as a result of the
confusion. The episode begins with Mary introducing
the item "writes articulately," and then her coding the
item: 316. After Mary states the item to be coded and
then what her code is, Anne responds with: "Oh,
that's what it says", with Lois rejoining: "No, that's
not what it says. . .". As you can see from the
transcript, the conversation is depicted temporally and
hierarchically, eg., Mary speaks, then Anne, then Lois,
then Mary and Gail momentarily speak at the same
time with Mary's statement continuing after Gail is
silent.

Each participant in the instance of social action
being transcribed is allocated two continuous lines.
On the top line, all verbal actions are presented and
on the second line all non-verbal gestures are
depicted. Further, the transcript is constructed in

65

Sample Transcript

Mary: "Writes Articulately" 3-1-6
       (writing and looking down at own papers)
Gail:
       (writing and looking down at own papers)
Lois:
       (writing and looking down at own papers)
Anne: Oh, that's what it
       (writing and looking down at own papers)

Mary:

Gail:

Lois: No, that's not what it says. "Writing and
           (looks up at M)   (looks at A)
Anne: says.   "Writing and

Mary: Oh, okay I put 3-1-6

Gail: Oh.   3-1-6

Lois: Articulating"   3-1-6

Anne: Articulating"   3-1-6

Mary: (laughs)   (laughs)

Gail: (laughs)   (laughs)
      (puts head down on table)
Lois: (laughs) I made a big deal out of that (laughs)
            (gestures at the air)   (looks at G)
Anne: (laughs)   (laughs)

66

Mary:

Gail:

Lois: No! It 's not writing and articulating, Mary,
    (raises voice mockingly, looks at M, pounds
Anne:

Mary:

Gail:

Lois: you jerk! You're screwing up the intercoder
    fist on table)
Anne:

Mary: And it's the only one on the page
              (looks at L)
Gail:

Lois: reliability (laughs)   on the page
                         (looks at G)
Anne:
                   (looks at M)

Mary: that we all agree on.   No.

Gail: It is, isn't it?
             (looks down at papers in
Lois: that we got right.   No. 2, 2, 2

Anne: No. 2 others.

Mary:

Gail: Where are they?   Friendly
    front of her)
Lois: others.   Yeah.

Anne: listening.

Mary: Clarity, and yeah, ones that have come
                                          (makes circular
Gail: Attitude.

Lois:

Anne:

Mary: up on every questionnaire (laugh)
       gesture with hands, looks at L)
Gail: There
                                                (points
Lois: Where?
                            (looks down at papers)
Anne:

Mary:

Gail: they are.
       at L's papers)
Lois: That's right.

Anne: .

such a way as to illustrate how the interactants are
"fitting" their behaviors together as well as how they
"build off" of one another to successfully produce
joint action. It is the "fitting" together of
sequential behavior that is the data for this
particular research. I will re-address this point
later in this chapter.

Participant Observation and Ethnography

> The concept of participant
> observation signifies the relation
> which the human observer of human
> beings cannot escape---having to
> participate in some fashion in the
> experience and action of those he
> observes. (Blumer, 1966: vi)

> The contribution of social
> anthropology may be to explore the
> structure of conversational
> interaction more directly and
> thoroughly, as part of ethnography,
> and to insist on understanding
> discourse structures as situated,
> that is, as pertaining to cultural
> and personal occasions which invest
> discourse with part of their
> meaning and structure. (Hymes,
> 1974:100)

As I've indicated the second type of data
generation technique used is naturalistic inquiry in
the form of participant observation. As Denzin (1970)
indicates naturalistic inquiry attempts to understand
the symbolic interaction, ongoing meaning construction,
and human social relationships that occur in everyday
or ordinary life. To do this degrees of participation
in the ongoing ordinary life situation is required.
This is so as participant observation status allows the
researcher "personal knowledge" of the interaction
patterns and histories of the group and its constituent
members. Subtleties in the group's interaction can be
detected by a participant observer more readily than by
a naive observer. While there are degrees of
participant observation stances, the one I have taken
is that of natural member. The stance adopted not only

has both advantages and disadvantages but is also directly related to issues of reliability.

Participant observers who are natural members of the groups studied are members before the research act is started. Here the research may be done either overtly or covertly. Since the research also employs video tape, the research act is overt. A natural tension emerges in this situation between the "objective" descriptive stand of the researcher and the "subjective" ongoing stand of the natural participant (Thorne, 1980, talks about this regarding her research on the anti-war/anti-draft movement of the late 1960's and early 1970's). This tension may hamper reliability, for at least two reasons. First, the question: "what blinders do you have on as a natural member?" must be addressed; and second a natural member must address: "what privileged information do you have as a natural member?" In other words, the natural member as a participant observer becomes aware of what she doesn't see because of closeness and what she does see because of closeness. There is a moral tenor to the second issue which isn't easily resolved. While all social acts are inherently public, not all public acts are public to all publics. Final decisions must, inevitably be personally made.

By merging participant observation with ethnographic videotape the advantages of data generated by only participant observation are overcome. Specifically, when an investigator generates data through participant observation, the data that are to be re-searched are field notes. The actual activity or action under investigation is transformed from naturally occuring behavior to notes about that behavior. By videotaping the data, interaction and not field notes are what are investigated.

This shift in data---from fieldnotes to videotaped interaction---in many ways eases some of the problems of reliability. Reliability requires little more than two or more people seeing the same thing. As Yarrow and Waxler (1979) state it: "Reliability of observational data is a question of agreement on what is 'registered' in independent observational records" (p.39). Few would argue that perception is interpretive and that there is no guarantee that any two people will see the same 'thing' regardless of

70

how concrete the object. Inter-subjectivity is even more fleeting when social life is being observed. Participant observation by itself requires that at the time of interaction observers see and code interaction in the same manner. By capturing social interaction, which is at best fleeting, on videotape, concrete "strips of social life" are made available for both participant and non-participant observers. The nature of videotape allows for processes of searching and re-searching. While participant observation is integral to data generation, a non-participant observation stand is, in part, adopted for the reliability measure, making the measure more robust.

Reliability

I employ a two-stage reliability measure with pre-test, test and test strategies. Two non-participants trained as inter-coders, the first as a pre-test reliability coder and the second as the reliability coder. Both the pre-test coder and reliability tester coded the same interaction presented to them on videotape. The tape used consisted of sixty-nine randomly selected "episodes" from the data being investigated. Three types of episodes emerge from the data and instances of these are represented on the reliability videotape. Coders were asked to code what type of episode occured as well as the sequential place of the episode on the tape. In all, the tape is forty-five minutes in length. After coding the three types of episodes and their sequential occurrence, the reliability test coder was presented with three episodes of fanciful recontextualization and was asked to code the sequence of events in each particular play episode. He was trained regarding "what fanciful recontextualization" was hypothesized to be as well as what concepts of "mutuality and "reciprocity" are.

Summary

Videotape, ethnography, and participant observation are singular generation methods typically employed by symbolic interactionists. Again, these data generation methods are acceptable because they meet the three criteria necessary for studying processual activity. They focus on naturally occuring interaction, provide known parameters which inform interactants of the consequences of their actions, and allow persons to formulate their own plans of action. From an interactionist standpoint these criteria are mandatory for the simple reason that it is upon these social occurrence that the theoretical base rests (Blumer, 1969; McPhail, 1977).

Symbolic Interaction as Methodological Perspective

A long standing distinction has been made within the enterprise of symbolic interaction between the Chicago and Iowa schools. These differences may be summarized as differences in methodological approaches to the study of social life. To this discussion what ultimately is important is the impact the methodological differences of these two strands of symbolic interaction theory have on what I call the new Iowa school of symbolic interaction. Meltzer and Petras (1970) make this theoretical distinction noteworthy when they contend that the bulk of symbolic interactionists work came out of either the Chicago school, led by Herbert Blumer, or the Iowa school, led by Manford Kuhn. From their point of view, the Chicago school paid serious attention to the study of social process while the Iowa school paid little or none. This is due to Kuhn's paper and pencil measure of the self---his Twenty Statements Test designed to get at, in the spirit of George Herbert Mead (1934), how the self is structured. Many, including Meltzer and Petras, think this to be antithetical to the writings of Mead (1934). Their criticism is based on the notion that one cannot make statements about the self, a fluid concept, by the use of a questionnaire. This assessment, however, is based solely on the content of Kuhn's research and not on the themes underlying his research.

While in many ways Kuhn's work stands in difference to Blumer's and Chicago school symbolic interaction, I will not delve into the specifics of what characterizes these schools of thought. Suffice it to say, Chicago school symbolic interaction emphasizes the processual nature of human life in theory and practice. Blumer's insistence on process is matched only by his emphasis that the researcher maintain a sort of fidelity between the ongoing world and her/his scientific actions in the world. For Blumer human process is concerted behavior. As he states it:

> The life of any human society consists necessarily of an ongoing process of fitting together the activities of its members. It is this complex of ongoing activity that establishes or portrays structure of organization (1969:7).

One of the questions becomes, then, if interactionists are to talk about process, if it is to become part of our universe of discourse, how is a way of seeing or frame of reference constructed that will enable researchers to agree with each other on what analysis is. On this point Blumer is of little help. His message is "go out and look." But as Buban (1979) points out social scientists ". . .who take process seriously have given up on Blumer's dictum. Many have solved this problem by concluding that the ability to 'see' process ranks with Carlos' ability to 'see' the mystical visions offered him by Don Juan" (1979:18). It is with this problem of "how to look at process" that Kuhn developed the TST. The consequences of this paper and pencil test impact greatly on the new Iowa school which offers data generation and data analysis techniques solving the problem of "how do we see process," or how do we observe the fitting together of human actions.

Kuhn's Iowa School Methodology

My work follows the analytical and theoretical lead of the New Iowa school of symbolic interaction. I see process by capturing slices of interaction on videotape and study process by combining the analytical concerns of Mead, Blumer, Kuhn, and Simmel. Burke's analytical pentad is also integral to my analysis, in particular as his analytical frame of reference is compatible with Mead's (1934) social act. Duncan (1962) discusses this compatibility at length and explicates:

> Like Mead, Burke argues that language determines society. It orders experience because it

creates the forms which make possible the communication of experience. He accepts. . .Mead's theory that the imagery of the end of an act, it's consummatory moment, determines how we form our attitude toward what we are about to do, and how we regard what we are doing, as we pass into the motor phase of the act. But for Burke this is only a first step. He wants to show how this consummatory moment arises in symbolic action (p.144).

Meltzer and Petras correctly argue that Kuhn ignored that basic features of human social life---interpersonal communication processes. His research tool, the Twenty Statements Test, was designed to analyze the structure of the self. This differed from other symbolic interactionist approaches in that it paid little attention to the notion of the self as a situationally shifting entity. Buban, however, notes that ". . . while Kuhn had more to offer both theoretically and methodologically than only the TST, most persons have come to treat his technique and the Iowa school as one and the same" (1979:12).

Aside from the content of Kuhn's work, an analysis of the form reveals that Kuhn sees the self as a social object present in all forms of human association and membership. It is the common denominator of all social activity and it is the only consistent variable present when human beings interact. To Kuhn, social life is structured self-reflecting life.

Kuhn's work intends to establish a methodological sophistication to the theories of symbolic interaction. Part of his work points to the irony that within the discipline the theoretical universe of discourse centers on the ideas of process and change while, in practice, these ideas are stagnant (1964). Kuhn assumes that the goal of symbolic interaction theory---to construct an empirically grounded theory---is far from accomplished. What the endeavor of symbolic interaction needs are coherent guidelines that allow processual theories to take on processual activities. While Kuhn does sacrifice a core concern

74

among interactionists (temporal process) he does develop ways to utilize some testable notions of empirical research (Buban, 1979).

In this light, Kuhn contributes three methodological dictums to symbolic interactionist thought. First, Kuhn contributes to interactionist thought the notion of selectivity---the deliberate and intentional bias of the researcher. Second, Kuhn, applies himself to a systematic analysis of data. Data is ordered by the researcher in a rigorous and non-speculative fashion. It is coherently arranged and elegantly communicated. Further, the notions of selectivity and systematizing lend to the researcher a status of active creator of the data s/he generates. In the spirit of interactionist thought, the researcher and subjects or participants, who also organize and create their own kind of data, have the same status.

Third, Kuhn maintains that the researcher must have a minimum of standpoints, that s/he must not only be selective in relation to the data, but also in location to the data. A researcher must intentionally narrow her/his focus in order to maintain one point of comparison or frame and continually go back to this frame to research it. To Kuhn, variegated standpoints preclude building a paradigmatic science in the sense that a researcher will never have the same frame of reference when s/he attempts to search and research a theoretical question.

Kuhn's work, as recognized by sympathetic observers, attempts to create interpersonal theories by applying scientific methods in order to ". . .build increasingly supported and dependable generalizations" (Buban, 1979:12). To borrow from another Kuhn (1962), his purpose was to create a normal science in order to move from a preparadigmatic to a paradigmatic status.

New Iowa School Methodology

The new Iowa school combines Kuhn's emphasis on systematic, selective, and point of view research with Blumer's insistence on process and on the active and interpretive human being. From this standpoint, people activate social processes and construct the concrete strips of behavior that provide researchers with

75

contexts for generating, recreating, analyzing and disseminating data in a more abstract sense (Hintz, 1974; Goffman, 1974; Geertz, 1974). As Miller (1978) notes:

> Social life takes its form and meaning through sequences of acts and interpretation of the participants. A systematic study of social life should take into account its processual-constructive nature, the acts, responses, and interpretations of the participants, and any patterns associated with these foci (p.19).

New Iowa school thought is build upon a structured/process perspective. In terms of this perspective, cooperative activity is seen in a hierarchical and sequential way ^{2}. Studies of processes are successful to the new Iowa school when they ". . .isolate the generic components of a particular social resultant, including the necessary and sufficient conditions of its occurrence as well as, potentially, the necessary sequence of these conditions" (Buban, 1979: 15). This analytical approach parallels on a social constructionist level the psychological structuralist approach of Piaget (1970).

The foundation of hierarchy and relationship is language, a system of shared plans of action. As Mead (1934) posits, language is based on the awareness and anticipation that a gesture (aural or visual) generates a response in another similar to that generated in the self. A relationship, then, is constructed when we can meaningfully anticipate others' responses in terms of how we would respond. Again, as Miller comments:

> The awareness of the potential responses to one's gestures allows for a system of shared response based on gestures, either through discourse or appearance. Through shared responses people can take a similar standpoint toward objects, acts and events. Awareness of self and definition of self come about when a person notes

the manner in which others act and respond toward him/her. The responses of and anticipated standpoint of others are taken into account in defining self and in the construction of social activities (1978: 20).

For the new Iowa school, all cooperative activity is based on language and communication. Anticipation and awareness of anticipations of programs of action and standpoints make cooperative activity possible. When we share plans of action and standpoints---when we publicly inform others of what we intend to do (verbally and nonverbally) and when we intend to locate ourselves to do it---we are cooperating to coordinate our activity. Two or more people who cooperate share a perspective of common standpoints while they construct courses of activity in order to reach a social objective.

The new Iowa school believes, then, that process can be explored by examining how people structure their interaction together. This structuring process can be sequentially arranged in a hierarchically dependent chain of necessary conditions. Relationships, the foundation of the school's paradigm, are constructed in this hierarchical way, or rather they are seen within a hierarchical frame of reference. Further, relationships are based upon the use of language. Language enables human beings to create meaningful slices of behavior and to construct and anticipate meaningful plans of action and standpoints vis-a-vis one another.

"Rather than ask how a particular structure alters a person's behavior, one asks how structuring is accomplished" (Buban, 1979: 16). Hence, new Iowa school symbolic interactionists would ask: how do persons construct solidarity relations, authority relations, or mutuality relationships. Another dimension of questioning would be: what are the features of particular forms of relationships, eg. what are the elements of or what comprise authority relationships or paternalistic relationships?

In order to generate data which gets at structured process, new Iowa school interactionists videotape

77

interacting human beings in a laboratory setting. They argue, as I have, that videotape captures all observable elements of human associations as they are being constructed. The experimental aspect of this type of research facilitates the relative ease of managing data compared to other data generating devises. Furthermore, in a laboratory setting the researcher creates the situation within which humans interact. By creating a specific situation for investigation, investigators have the advantage of understanding the situation. This understanding simplifies the investigators task; by holding the situation constant external variables which may affect the interaction are minimized. Lastly, in a laboratory setting investigators are able to create comparison groups.

Nevertheless, there are problems with the use of a laboratory for the generation of data. Sehested and Couch (1978) identify a laboratory setting as authoritarian. Specifically, the relationship constructed between the researchers and the participants in the study or experiment is an authoritarian one as the researchers impose constraints on the interactants. These constraints create the possibility of undesirable results. Participants in laboratory settings or studies may organize themselves to act as the experimenter wants them to "for the sake of science" (Milgarm, 1974; Orne, 1962). In this light, three alternative data generation techniques were selected for this study. And these have already been discussed.

While the data generation techniques selected for this study depart from those used by new Iowa school symbolic interactionists, the data analysis procedures do not. While these procedures are introduced in chapter one, I will elaborate on them here.

Data Analysis Procedure

New Iowa school symbolic interactionists engage in a unique method of theory generation. Theory generation from this standpoint is intimately intertwined with the central concerns of forms of association and social relationships as described by Simmel (1950). Generic processes can be identified specifying the reciprocal acts of the interactants and then identifying the sequential order of those acts. It is assumed that the critical features of the theory would describe all cases of the data.

The collection, coding and analysis of the data are not simultaneous activities as they are in the more familiar method of theory generation: the procedure of grounded theory (Glasser and Strauss, 1967). The coding and analysis of the data, however, are simultaneous and dynamic activities.

There are three objectives to this method of theory generation. First, to identify the reciprocal acts of people as they engage in joined or concerted behavior, ie., the social process of producing accounts (Lutfiyya and Miller 1986), negotiating (Couch and Sink, 1980), and authority (Miller, 1979). To identify these reciprocal acts attention is paid to both the verbal and non-verbal communication of interacting persons. Two assumptions are made when identifying or delineating reciprocal activity: 1) that social action involves at least a dyad; and 2) that persons are minded and capable of covert behaviors (Mead, 1934). The unit of analysis, thus, is at least an interacting dyad and the unit of observation is reciprocal activity. Coding schemes focus on how persons fit their behavior together in a concerted fashion. Facilitating the observation of fitting behavior together are both videotaped interaction and transcriptions of the interaction.

Sensitizing concepts (Blumer, 1955) are generated which describe the generic nature of the activity under investigation, eg., mutual responsiveness or congruent functional identities^3. These concepts identify the simultaneous and reciprocal acts which are meaningfully joined by persons concerting behavior (within the situational parameters of the generated data).

Even though the assumption is made that social activities produced by human beings are minded, the coding and analysis of the data focus only on public activity. Hence, only observable acts are coded and analyzed (Couch, 1975).

A second objective of this method of theory generation is the specification of the order in which the reciprocal acts identified are constructed. This is necessary to understand the processual nature of the concerted activity. To specify the order in which reciprocal acts occur, acts are noted in terms of their occurrence in relation to each other. Even during the early stages of analysis, before the reciprocal acts are clearly specified, the coordination of interactants' behavior is noted. The specification of ordered activity has parallels in analytic induction (Turner, 1953).

The third objective of this method is to generate a theory which can explain <u>all</u> the cases of the data. This ongoing method of theory construction emphasizes the developing and reformulating of the theory in light of any negative cases which appear in the data being analyzed.

The coding and analysis of the data begins with a specific question: How do persons create contexts through play? In order to thoroughly understand any process of human interaction an analysis similar to Geertz's (1974) thick description is used [4].

While using the method of thick description a series of fluid hypotheses are developed and investigated by comparing each instance of the data. Each episode of fanciful recontextualization is compared with all other episodes of fanciful recontextualization, and this comparison culminates in hypotheses about the nature of how fanciful recontextualization takes place. These hypotheses consist of specific ideas about the exact reciprocal acts that are being produced as well as the specific ordering of those acts. These hypotheses are continually evaluated in relation to the data observed. When data are found that do not support a hypothesis that has been generated, then a new hypothesis, including all known facts, is formulated. As anomalies appear, the developing theory is modified to include them. Common features are gradually discovered such that the same "hypothesis" describing instance one of fanciful recontextualization will also describe instances three and five.

The generation of theory, using this method, consists of an ongoing dynamic process. As such the theory of fanciful recontextualization produced must not be approached as a static structure limited to testing and minor reformulation.

The next chapter, "Results and Analysis," presents my theory of context creation. Transcripts of interaction are the data analyzed and presented. The results of the reliability test are also presented and discussed in Chapter Five.

Endnotes

1. The basic format for the TST is a series of twenty blank lines that the subject fills out with answers to the question: "Who am I?", eg. a graduate student, the sound of one hand clapping, the Walrus, etc. . Answers are basically coded as to whether they indicate consensual (responses that other's in the subject's environment can readily share) or non-consensual replies. These responses get at one's self-concept and other's conception of self as well.

2. The notion of hierarchy implies a movement from a more general and least complex type of activity to more specific and complex activities. General is used in a pragmatic way, indicating possibilities, eg. when humans begin interaction there are several possible directions for the interaction to take, these directions narrow as choices are made, futures projected, and commitments to certain lines of action are made. A study of openings by Miller, Hintz and Couch (1975) demonstrates this hierarchical notion. In order for two people to move from independent to interdependent lines of action, they must reciprocally acknowledge one another's attention (eg. make eye contact), be mutually responsive, share a focus, and project a future toward a shared objective. In order to project a future, the previous steps must be accomplished. All of the steps may happen simultaneously and often do between persons who have extended personal histories with one another as friends or lovers do.

3. Mutual responsiveness occurrences when: "One is responsive to another and when he builds his acts off the prior, simultaneous, or anticipated acts of another, and in the process of so doing informs the other participant(s) of the fact" (Miller,et al.,1975).

   Congruent functional identities are: "present when both parties impute to self and other sequences of forthcoming behavior" (Scheff, 1970).

4. Thick description is a methodological device used by some anthropologists. It involves the detailed inspection and description of public social activity. From a number of cases generalizations are.

C H A P T E R   F I V E

Results and Analysis

> As the contemporary artists
> Gene Davis put it, "context is
> content" (1971: 39). The
> significance of the vowel arises
> from surrounding vowels, a word
> from its ties to other words, a
> sentence from its position in an
> argument. Human acts are embedded
> in a hierarchy of contexts such
> that each frames and thereby
> influences the meanings that arise
> within it. (Barnlund, 1981:108)

Introduction

A six stage sequence of fanciful
recontextualization was isolated beginning with a focus
jump from the mundane and culminating in the
restoration of everyday life. In more detail, the
structured process of fanciful recontextualization
entails in sequence: jump focus, focus acceptance,
focus elaboration, re-introduction of the mundane as
primary focus, acceptance of the re-introduced focus,
and restoration of everyday life (this structured
process is illustrated on page 115).

A detailed discussion of the analysis of the
structured process of fanciful recontextualization will
be presented after a more general description of the
data in its entirety. By describing the data as a whole
a more exact and accurate understanding of the process
of fanciful recontextualization is possible. Included
in this discussion are the results of the reliability
test.

Reliability was established in two-stages using
naive coders (naive meaning non-participants who were
unfamiliar with the research project). One stage
involved coding the types of episodes isolated from the
data while the other stage involved coding the
structured process of fanciful recontextualization that
was isolated from the data. Reliability regarding the

structured process of fanciful recontextualization will be reported first followed by that of the isolated episode types.

Reliability of the Structured Process of Fanciful Recontextualization

The reliability coder for this study was asked to look at video recordings of three episodes of fanciful recontextualization. Before doing this he was "trained" to understand mutuality and reciprocity in regards to a symbolic interactionists notion of behavior as "fitting" together. Training was facilitated by the coder's familiarity with Blumer's concept of joint action (and although the reliability coder was an academic, he did not identify himself as a symbolic interactionist).

This part of the reliability test was twofold. First, a "description" was solicited from the reliability coder; and second, the reliability coder was instructed to code the sequential and ordered elements of fanciful recontextualization. I will briefly elaborate on both of these aspects of the reliability testing procedures.

Regarding the first aspect of this stage of the reliability test, immediately prior to coding the elements of the structured process of fanciful recontextualization, the reliability coder was asked to "describe" in his own words what fanciful recontextualization appeared to be like. As he described it, fanciful recontextualization was: "a climatic event where the playful interaction built-up and then ceased."

The second aspect of this part of the reliability testing involved a "structured" coding procedure. Specifically, while viewing the videotapes, the reliability coder was instructed to code the interaction according to the six sequential elements isolated as the process of fanciful recontextualization. The coding procedure involved detecting both if the feature occured (if "jump focus" occured or if "focus elaboration" occured) and when exactly the feature occured (what specific behavioral referent was the isolated feature).

84

In all three instances of fanciful recontextualization the coding of the reliability coder matched the researcher's analysis.

Isolated Episode Type Reliability

Throughout this analysis "episodes" are operationally defined as communicative routines which are distinct wholes, distinguished from other types of discourse by clearly recognizable openings and closings. The video taped data revealed three types of interaction episodes or social acts: normal episodes, elaborated episodes, and fanciful episodes. In total 298 episodes naturally occured. Normal episodes were the most prevalent (as such earning their name as normal) in the ethnographic data generated to study the structured process of fanciful recontextualization (n=165). Elaborated episodes were the next most prevalent (n=122), while fanciful social acts occured the least frequently of the three (n=11). I will describe these episode types in detail after reporting the reliability results.

Two non-participants trained as inter-coder reliability raters, the first as a "development" reliability coder and the second as the "final" reliability coder. Specifically, the first coder was trained separately from and prior to the final reliability coder. From her coding and "insights" changes were made in the discussion and description of the coding scheme when training the final reliability coder. Both of the coders judged the same interaction presented to them on videotape. The tape consisted of sixty-nine randomly selected "episodes" from the data being investigated. Neither the development coder nor the final coder were told how many episodes were on the tape.

Coders were instructed to code the type of episode that occured as well as the sequential placing of the episode on the tape. In other words, they had to sequentially number the episodes as well as to code the type of episodic interaction. Having reliability coders indicate the sequential placing of episodes was important for two reasons. First, the sequential

85

placement of episodes was coded in order to avoid an "accidental" similarity in the coding of simply the amount of episodes per category. By ensuring that the number of coded episodes per category are similar or dissimilar intentionally (and not accidentally) reliability is enhanced. Second, coding the sequential placement of episodes allows for the determination of any patterns in the coding disagreement among coders and between single or individual coders and the actual taped and coded data. Patterns of disagreement facilitate questions regarding the training of reliability coders as well as the coding scheme itself.

In all, the reliability tape was forty-five minutes long and consisted of 39 normal episodes, 21 elaborated episodes, and 9 fanciful episodes. Table 1 reports the results of the reliability test in terms of the number of episodes per category that were detected by the development and final reliability coders. In the table these results are contrasted with the tape as coded by the researcher. Table 2 presents the per episode code of the development reliability coder contrasted with the tape per episode code as established by the researcher. Code agreement by episode is indicated and total percent agreement, normal episode agreement, elaborated episode agreement, and fanciful episode agreement are presented. Table 3 contains the same information for the final reliability coder in contrast to the coded reliability tape. For Tables 2 and 3, percent agreement is the number of episodes per category that are coded identically by the researcher and the naive coder (for Table 2 the naive coder is the development reliability coder and for Table 3 the naive coder is the final reliability coder) divided by the total per category episodes that are coded by both the specific reliability coder and the researcher. Total percent agreement is the sum of episodes coded the same way by the reliability tape and the naive coder divided by the total number of reliability tape episodes.

As Table 2 indicates, the sum of the normal episodes detected by the development coder and the researcher is 44 with 28 code agreements, 28 elaborated episodes with 9 agreements, and 20 fanciful episodes with 9 code agreements. Calculated total percent agreement is 67%, normal episode agreement 64%, elaborated episode agreement 32%, and fanciful episode

TABLE 1

Of Episodes Per Category
By
Coders and Reliability Tape

TYPE OF EPISODE

		Normal	Elaborated	Fanciful
C O D E R S T A T U S	Develop-ment Coder	33	16	20
	Final Coder	39	21	9
	Tape	39	21	9

ACTUAL # OF EPISODES = 69

TABLE 2

DEVELOPMENT RELIABILITY CODING

Episode Number	Reliability Tape Code	Development Coder	Agreement (+)
1	F	F	+
2	E	E	+
3	F	F	+
4	N	N	+
5	N	E	
6	N	N	+
7	N	N	+
8	N	N	+
9	E	N	
10	N	E	
11	N	N	+
12	N	N	+
13	N	N	+
14	E	E	+
15	E	E	+
16	F	F	+
17	E	E	+
18	N	N	+
19	N	N	+
20	N	N	+
21	N	N	+
22	E	E	+
23	N	N	+
24	E	N	
25	N	E	
26	N	N	+
27	N	N	+
28	N	N	+
29	E	N	
30	N	E	

Episode Number	Reliability Tape Code	Development Coder	Agreement (+)
31	N	N	+
32	F	F	+
33	E	N	
34	N	F	
35	E	N	
36	N	E	
37	N	N	+
38	N	E	
39	N	F	
40	F	F	+
41	E	F	
42	E	F	
43	N	N	+
44	E	F	
45	N	N	+
46	F	F	+
47	N	N	+
48	E	E	+
49	F	F	+
50	E	F	
51	E	F	
52	N	N	+
53	N	N	+
54	E	E	+
55	N	N	+
56	N	F	
57	N	N	+
58	N	N	+
59	F	F	+
60	N	F	
61	E	E	+
62	N	N	+
63	P	F	
64	P	F	
65	P	P	+
66	F	F	+
67	N	N	+
68	N	P	
69	N	N	+

Note. Proportional Total Agreement is .66, proportional Normal Episode Agreement is .72, proportional Elaborated Agreement is .42, and proportional Fanciful Episode Agreement is 1.00.

TABLE 3

FINAL RELIABILITY

Episode Number	Reliability Tape Code	Final Code	Agreement (+)
1	F	F	+
2	E	E	+
3	F	F	+
4	N	E	
5	N	N	+
6	N	N	+
7	N	N	+
8	N	N	+
9	E	E	+
10	N	N	+
11	N	N	+
12	N	N	+
13	N	N	+
14	E	E	+
15	E	E	+
16	F	F	+
17	E	E	+
18	N	N	+
19	N	N	+
20	N	N	+
21	N	N	+
22	E	E	+
23	N	N	+
24	E	N	
25	N	E	
26	N	N	+
27	N	N	+
28	N	N	+
29	E	E	+
30	N	N	+

Episode Number	Reliability Tape Code	Final Code	Agreement (+)
31	N	N	+
32	F	F	+
33	E	N	
34	N	N	+
35	E	E	+
36	N	N	+
37	N	N	+
38	N	N	+
39	N	N	+
40	F	F	+
41	E	E	+
42	E	N	
43	N	N	+
44	E	E	+
45	N	E	
46	F	F	+
47	N	N	+
48	E	E	+
49	F	F	+
50	E	E	+
51	E	E	+
52	N	N	+
53	N	N	+
54	E	E	+
55	N	N	+
56	N	N	+
57	N	N	+
58	N	N	+
59	F	F	+
60	N	N	+
61	E	E	+
62	N	N	+
63	E	E	+
64	E	E	+
65	E	E	+
66	F	F	+
67	N	N	+
68	N	N	+
69	N	N	+

Note. Proportional Total Agreement is .91, proportional Normal Episode Agreement is .92, proportional Elaborated Agreement is .86, and proportional Fanciful Episode Agreement is 1.00.

agreement 45%. Proportional agreements for total
agreement, normal episode agreement, elaborated
episode agreement and fanciful episode agreement were
also calculated and reported in Tables 2 and 3. The
calculated proportional agreements were used to
calculate a Scott's π , a statistic which was
developed "to improve the accuracy of content analysis
and get some measure of the extent of inter-coder
agreement. . ." (Scott,1955: 321). As Scott (1955)
explains, this statistic "corrects for the
number of categories in the code, and the frequency
with which each is used. In the practical coding
situation it varies from 0.00 to 1.00, regardless of
the number of categories in the dimension, and is thus
comparable with the "percentage agreement" figure"
(p.323). The Scott's π calculated for the
development reliability coding was .40.

When analyzing the fanciful episodes agreed upon,
the development reliability coder detected all nine
fanciful episodes. However, this coder also coded 11
other episodes as fanciful.

Seven of the 11 "extra" fanciful episodes are
elaborated episodes where either a joke is told or
where "laughing" takes place. As already determined,
fanciful recontextualization involves more than simply
the telling of a joke or mutual laughter. What this
coding indicates is "insufficient" coder training.

Based on these "development" reliability
results, modifications were made to the final
reliability test coder's training. Specifically,
accompanying a brief description of each of the episode
types, the inter-coder for the reliability test was
shown a videotaped example of each of the isolated
episodes. In contrast to the development reliability,
the final reliability percentage agreements were much
higher as was the calculated Scott's π .

As Table 1 reports, the number of episodes per
category detected by the final reliability coder and
the researcher are identical. Discrepancies, however,
emerge in the coding of actual or individual episodes.
All the disagreements occur between the coding of
normal and elaborated episodes since the 9 fanciful
episodes which appeared on the reliability tape are

coded as such (as fanciful episodes) by the reliability test coder.

Percentage agreements (see Table 3) between the final reliability coder and the researcher are 91% for overall agreement, 86% for normal episode agreement, 75% for elaborated episode agreement, and 100% for fanciful episode agreement. The calculated Scott's π was .84.

Undoubtedly, the most important reliability result is the 100% agreement between the reliability tester and the researcher regarding the fanciful episodes. With that attention turns to an in-depth description of the isolated episode types from the data analyzed.

Isolated Episode Types

Even though the emphasized concern is with the episodes of play, two reasons stand out as important for noting the two other episode types. Once stated, these reasons frame a comparative discussion of the three types of episodes. First, normal and elaborated episodes provide a naturally emergent contrast to the episodes of play. Naturally emergent contrasts allow for a more precise image of fanciful recontextualization. Second, given that the play develops from and recontextualizes the mundane or the serious, understanding the recontextualization process requires understanding what the serious ongoing interaction patterns are.

Normal Episodes

Normal episodes are quite short in duration and involve the completion of the coding of a single questionnaire item. Of the four normal episodes presented in transcribed form here, the longest lasted 12 seconds while the shortest was 6 seconds in duration. Recall that the ethnographic data generated was a non-continuous five hour videotape of a four-woman research team who were content analyzing and coding the open-ended questionnaire responses to a survey on women's perceptions of their own communication. Very simply, the following transcript (see Figure B) illustrates two sequential normal episodes.

93

FIGURE B

Sequential Normal Episode

Mary: "Listens" 1-2-3
        (reading from papers in front of her and coding)
Gail: 1-2-3
        (reading from papers in front of her and coding)
Lois: 1-2-3
        (reading from papers in front of her and coding)
Anne: 1-2-3
        (reading from papers in front of her and coding)

Mary: "Concisely," 2-1-6
        (reading from papers in front of her and coding)
Gail: 2-1-6
        (reading from papers in front of her and coding)
Lois: 2-1-6
        (reading from papers in front of her and coding)
Anne: 2-1-6
        (reading from papers in front of her and coding)

In both episodes, Mary begins the coding procedure by introducing the questionnaire item response which is "listens" in the first instance and "concisely" in the second. After stating the questionnaire response, Mary states how she coded the item along the three dimensions being examined. Immediately after her, Anne then Lois and lastly Gail state how they coded the questionnaire response (when coding "listens" all researchers coded the item 1-2-3). A normal episode occurs when no discussion of the coding takes place. While the examples in Figure B illustrate an episode where "listens" is coded 1-2-3 by all of the members of the research team, not all normal episodes have questionnaire item responses coded the same way by all of the participants. For instance the next two transcripts (Figure C) are of normal episodes where in the first case research group members coded "enthusiastically" different from one another and where in the second instance "presenting workshops" is coded differently.

Elaborated Episodes

Elaborated episodes, differing from normal episodes, emerge when some discussion of the coding or ongoing research task takes place. The discussion which occurs in prolonged episodes just as the lack of discussion in the normal episodes represents "the serious" interaction patterns of the data base. The following transcript illustrates a prolonged episode (Figure D). In contrast to the normal episodes of Figure B and Figure C this prolonged episode is 106 seconds in duration.

"Eye contact" is the item being coded and it becomes an issue for discussion when the research team member Lois realizes that she has coded the item differently from the other three researchers. A discussion of the coding procedure for "eye contact" ensues until Lois finds a similarity coded item on a previously compiled list of codes. Once this has happened Mary introduces another code for the next questionnaire item response (by saying 2-1-7).

While the transcript in Figure D is 106 seconds long, the following elaborated episode (Figure E) is only 15 seconds long. This transcript is presented to

.

95

FIGURE C

Normal Episodes With Questionnaire
Response Items Coded Differently
By Group Members

Mary: Um,"enthusiastically," 1-1-7
        (looks down at papers and codes response)
Gail: 3-1-4
        (looks down at papers and codes response)
Lois: 3-1-7
        (looks down at papers and codes response)
Anne: 3-1-7
        (looks down at papers and codes response)

Mary: "Presenting workshops," 2-2-2
        (looks down at papers and codes response)
Gail: 3-1-6
        (looks down at papers and codes response)
Lois: 3-2-6
        (looks down at papers and codes response)
Anne: 3-2-8
        (looks down at papers and codes response)

FIGURE D

Elaborated Episode

```
Mary:  Okay, 1-2-2
       (looks down at papers and writes)
Gail:
       (looks down at papers and writes)
Lois:                  What did you say?      Oh God!
       (looks down at papers and writes)
Anne:            1-2-2                  1-2-2
       (looks down at papers and writes)


Mary:
       (continues looking down at papers) (looks at L)
Gail:        1-2-2              Yeah, it was one that we
       (continues looking at papers) (looks at L)
Lois:  1-1-2      Did I screw?
       (starts looking through papers)
Anne:
       (continues looking at papers) (looks at 1)


Mary:

Gail:  talked about.                Um Hum.  We said
                                    (continues looking
Lois:              Are you serious?

Anne:
                            (looks at G)


Mary:                                     Uh Huh.

Gail:  that "eye contact" was other-centered.
       at L)
Lois:

Anne:
```

Mary: But it's not on our list. . . .

Gail: Yeah,

Lois: Is it on here?
       (continues looking through papers)
Anne:

Mary:
                     (EC=G)
Gail: but I struggled with it because "with eyes"
                     (EC=M)
Lois:

Anne:

Mary:

Gail: could mean not necessarily "eye contact," I had

Lois:

Anne: .

Mary: I just, I just

Gail: a, these really drove me nuts (laughs)
            (looks at A and then L)
Lois:

Anne:

Mary: we had "eye contact and smile" under "other"
                                        (looks at A)
Gail:

Lois:

Anne: "other"
                                    (looks at m)

Mary: and so I said, I assumed that everyone would
                     (looks at G and then L)
Gail:

Lois:

Anne:

Mary: look on the list and see "eye contact" and

Gail:

Lois:

Anne:

Mary: put it down.

Gail: Yeah.
           (looks at M)
Lois: I don't, it's not on my list.
           (continues looking through
Anne:

Mary:

Gail: It's on my list.
    (looks at L)
Lois: Do you see it?
    papers)   (leans over to A)
Anne: "Look at and
                     (points to

Mary:

Gail:

Lois: Where? Oh that! "Looks at and smile"
        (leans back into chair and looks up)
Anne: smile"
papers)

Mary:

Gail: But we talked about "eye
                               (looks at L, then M, and then
Lois: that's one thing.

Anne:

Mary: Yeah!
                                             (looks at G)
Gail: contact" as "other-centered."
         A)
Lois: We did? Oh
                                                 (looks down
Anne: Yeah!
                                             (looks at G)

Mary: 2-1-7
         (looks down at papers)
Gail: Wait 'til you hear the answers
                 (looks down at papers)
Lois: crap! (loud sigh)
         at papers)
Anne: .
         (looks down at papers)

Mary:

Gail: on this one (ha, ha, ha).

Lois:

Anne:

Elaborated Episode of Short Duration

```
Mary:  Okay, 3-2-6
       (writing and looking down at own papers)
Gail:                          3-2-6   What? Have we
       (writing and looking down at own papers) (looks
Lois:                 1-2-5
       (writing and looking down at own papers)
Anne:                 3-2-6
       (writing and looking down at own papers)

Mary:

Gail:  agreed on two so far?                      Oh.
       at L's papers and leans toward her)
Lois:                     Three,no, two totally.
                 (continues looking at own papers)
Anne:                                        Yeah.
```

illustrate that it is not actual clock time which
determines if an episode is considered elaborated or
normal but that it is the amount of conversation which
allows for this determination.

In both the normal and elaborated episodes which
emerged the act of conducting research occurs within
the scene of a university and doing the business of
academics. The agency involved is the coding of
questionnaire item responses by actors or agents who
are researchers and academics. The purpose, in its
broadest sense, of the act is to answer researchable
questions about women's perceptions of their own
communication. Normal and elaborated episodes are
structurally similar in that the purpose and agency as
enacted by the agents allow for the scene to contain
the act.

In contrast to normal and elaborated episodes, in
the episodes of fanciful recontextualization as they
are enacted by the agents or actors, the purpose and
agency allow for the act to contain the scene. When
act contains scene, recontextualization has taken
place. This will be developed on in the upcoming
discussion of the general characteristics of fanciful
recontextualization episodes.

Fanciful Episodes

Fanciful episodes are episodes where social play
"breaks out." When these episodes emerge, the
participants put their ongoing serious activity into
another context and comment on the activity from this
perspective. The transcript in Figure F is an example
of fanciful recontextualization.

This episode of fanciful recontextualization
begins with the serious sounding statement by Gail:
"Yeah, women are sorry creatures who lack skills but
who give of themselves." Even though the tone of voice
used by Gail sounds serious, its intended playfulness
is revealed when Gail begins laughing and Mary, Lois,
and Anne join in.

Gail introduces this "playful" frame as a comment
on Mary's previous statement that all of the negative
characteristics that have appeared as open-ended

102

FIGURE F

Fanciful Episode

Mary: If you look at the list of all of the bad or
(looks down at papers)

Gail:
(looks down at papers)

Lois:
(looks down at papers)

Anne:
(looks down at papers)

Mary: negative characteristics are coded female.

Gail: Yeah,
(serious

Lois:

Anne:

Mary:

Gail: women are sorry creatures who lack skills but
sounding voice, looks at L, EC=L)

Lois:
(EC=G)

Anne:

Mary: (laughs) That's what it sounds
(leans back in chair,

Gail: who give of themselves (laughs)
(looks at M)

Lois: (laughs)

Anne: (laughs)

Mary: like you. . .
looks at G and then L)

Gail:

Lois: Women are (pause) we'll write it,
(looks at m)

Anne:
(looks down at own papers)

103

Mary: That

Gail:

Lois: this in our paper. Women are sorry creatures

Anne:

Mary: should be the first line in the introduction
         (continues looking at L)
Gail:

Lois:

Anne:

Mary: (laughs)

Gail:

Lois:

Anne: (laughs) Women are (pause) and we have evidence

Mary: This is
                                                  (looks
Gail:

Lois: (laughs) Yes we can prove that.
                                 (looks down at own papers)
Anne: to prove it (laughs)

Mary: research done by women, so, of course, sexism
         down at own papers)
Gail:

Lois:

Anne:

```
Mary:    can't be an issue

Gail:                be an issue, right, sexist? me?
                     (looks down at own papers)
Lois:

Anne:


Mary:    Women aren't sexist (laughs) right.

Gail:                          (laughs)

Lois:                          (laughs)

Anne:                          (laughs)  Uhh, okay, so
                                         (looks down at

Mary:

Gail:

Lois:

Anne:    we had done. . .
         own papers)
```

question responses have been coded as "female" by the researchers.

Once all of the participants understand the frame set by Gail's statement, they build-off of it, transcend the serious and "comment" on two important issues. First, the stereotypical perceptions of women's communication is "made fun of." Second, the notion that women are not sexist, or more importantly cannot be sexist is commented on.

Figure G presents a second illustration of an episode of fanciful recontextualization. While in the first example (Figure F) very little conversation leads up to the emergence of play or playfulness, in this second example, play takes a much longer time to emerge and is more fleeting once it has. As in the previous example, Gail introduces the playful frame. She does so when she says: " . . . I have great sensitivity toward the starving children of the world (laugh), but I don't communicate with them." While everyone laughs when Gail does (as indicated on the transcript), the mutual laughter is not sufficient to define an episode as an instance of fanciful recontextualization. This episode . becomes one of fanciful recontextualization when Mary, while laughing, builds off of Gail's playful frame by saying: "And you don't send them your dinner leftovers or cry when. . . ." Lois also verbally builds off of the initial playful statement when she says: I don't think you have any sensitivity toward the starving children of the world."

In other words, for fanciful recontextualization to emerge the other participants must not only recognize the "playfulness" of the initiated frame but they must build-off of the frame. By building on the playful frame, the initial statement moves from the status of joke or joking to the status of playing.

Anne is the one who ends the recontextualized episode by saying: ". . .I put it there because understanding is one of the receptive skills so if you try to understand others. . .". By not only saying this but by having the statement accepted as the next conversation focus, the scene of "doing research" is re-established as the container of the act of "coding questionnaire responses." Once the scene again contains the act, ordinary social life is restored.

Fanciful Recontextualization

Mary: "Tries to put self in others situation" 1-2-5
      (reading from papers in front of her)
Gail:
      (looking at papers in front of her)
Lois:
      (looking at papers in front of her)
Anne:
      (looking at papers in front of her)

Mary:

Gail: No, I
                                            (looks
Lois: 1-2-5
                (EC=A)
Anne: 1-2-3   um, well, being understood
               (EC=L) (looks at G, gestures with hands)

Mary: Yeah, taking the role of the other
                    (looks down at own papers)
Gail: think so   Yeah
      at A)
Lois:
                                            (looks
Anne:

Mary:

Gail: I said 1-2-5 but if you're going to talk about
                    (EC=A)
Lois:
      down at own papers)
Anne:
                    (EC=G)

Mary:

Gail: reception skills empathy is considered one in

Lois:

Anne:

Mary:

Gail: the literature, I mean I coded it 1-2-5 'cause

Lois:

Anne:
                                                    (looks

Mary:
                              (looks at G)
Gail: I made reception skills very narrow, but we've
                                              (looks at
Lois:

Anne:
      at G and then M)

Mary:
                              (looks down at own
Gail: got a real problem with this category in terms
      M)   (looks down at own
Lois:
                              (looks down at own
Anne: .
                              (looks down at own

Mary: Yeah, um 'cause if you read it as
      papers)
Gail: of definition
      papers)
Lois:
      papers)
Anne:
      papers)

Mary: sensitive it can

Gail:

Lois: No, no, it doesn't say
                              (looking down at own
Anne:
                              (looking down at own

Mary:

Gail: But if you can put yourself

Lois: sensitive (pause)
        papers)
Anne:
        papers)

Mary:

Gail: in the role of the other

Lois: But it says tries to
                             (reading from own papers)
Anne:

Mary:

Gail: That's putting
                                     (looks at L)
Lois: put self in others situation

Anne:

Mary:

Gail: yourself in the role of the other.

Lois: No, I
                                         (looks up at
Anne:
                                         (looks at G

Mary:

Gail:

Lois: understand but when we said a reception skill
        M, then G)
Anne:
        and then L)

Mary:

Gail:

Lois: presumably that's something that's going on

Anne:

Mary:

Gail: huh, um but
                                        (looks at L)
Lois: during the communication process

Anne:

Mary:
                                    (EC=G)
Gail: don't you use empathy during the communication
                                    (EC=M)
Lois:

Anne:

Mary:

Gail: process?

Lois: Well, you can say empathy but you can

Anne:

Mary: Yeah, I'm sure this
                                        (EC=A, smiles)
Gail:

Lois: have empathy outside of the

Anne:
                                        (EC=M, smiles)

110

Mary: person isn't thinking about it in terms of

Gail:

Lois:

Anne:

Mary: George Herbert Mead's definition of the meaning

Gail:

Lois:

Anne:

Mary: of the word.

Gail: .   But I can have great sensitivity
                                (EC=L)
Lois:
                                (EC=G)
Anne:

Mary:

Gail: toward the needs of others outside of the

Lois:

Anne:

Mary:

Gail: communication system too, I mean, I have great

Lois:

Anne:

Mary:
                        (looks at G)

Gail: sensitivity toward the starving children of the

Lois:

Anne:
                            (looks at G)

Mary: (laugh)

Gail: world (laugh) but I don't communicate with
                  (looks down at own papers)
Lois: (laugh)
                (looks at G)
Anne: (laugh)
                (looks at G)

Mary: (laughing) And you don't send them your

Gail: them (laughing)

Lois: (laughing)

Anne: (laughing)

Mary: dinner leftovers or cry when. . .

Gail: (laughing)

Lois: (laughing) I don't think you have any

Anne: (laughing)

Mary:

Gail:

Lois: sensitivity toward the starving children of the
                      (looks at A)
Anne:

Mary: How many starving children do you
           (looks at G, EC=G)
Gail:
                      (EC=M)
Lois: world.

Anne:

Mary: support?

Gail:

Lois:

Anne: I, I put it there because understanding
               (looking through own papers)

Mary:

Gail:

Lois: ˙

Anne: is one of the reception skills so if . . .

Structured Process of
Fanciful Recontextualization

The structured process of fanciful recontextualization encompasses jump focus, focus acceptance, focus elaboration, re-introduction of the mundane as the primary focus, acceptance of the re-introduced focus, and the restoration of everyday life. These features of fanciful recontextualization are: 1) necessary and ordered, and 2) elements of reciprocal activity. Figure H (see next page) diagrams the structured process of fanciful recontextualization. This diagram assumes that fanciful recontextualization is a social act. Mead (1934) and those who followed him (e.g., Kuhn, 1962; Myiamoto, 1970; and Couch, 1979) would find this characterization compatible with Mead's (1934) definition of a social act. Afterall, the necessary and ordered features of a social act are openings, middles, and closings.

To elaborate, interactants must verbally or non-verbally create all of the necessary processual characteristics of fanciful recontextualization for a context shift to take place. When social actors sequentially enact these necessary steps, ordering is accomplished.

Additionally, reciprocal activity is the foundation of Mead's (1934) notion of social action. "A person purchasing an object in a store is not producing social action; nor is a person selling objects producing social action. It is only when they join their activities to make an exchange that they are involved in the production of social action" (Hintz, 1974:47). While social action can range from the very simple (e.g., purchasing a pack of gum from a salesclerk) to the very complex (e.g., Sadat and Begin debating the possibility of "peace" between Egypt and Israel), at its heart is the joined or concerted behavior which is reciprocal action.

"Openings" (Miller, 1975) to any social act encompass minimal reciprocal action. While there are three necessary and ordered features to openings---the establishment of reciprocally acknowledged attention, the establishment of mutual responsiveness, and the establishment of congruent functional identities---only the last is of concern here. The reasoning for this is

114

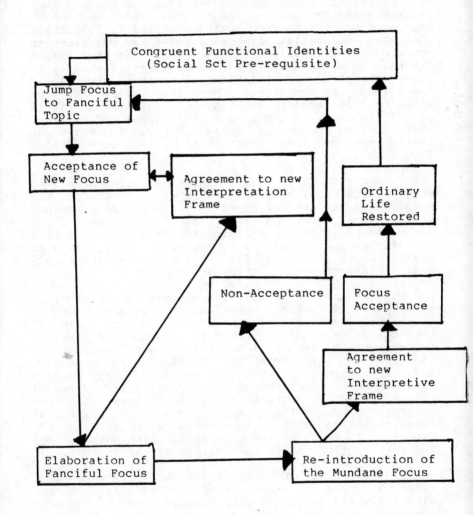

FIGURE H

The Structured Process of
Fanciful Recontextualization

simple. Since the elements of openings form a hierarchy (a consequence of the elements being necessary and ordered) the last element, congruent functional identities, assumes the earlier two elements.

Congruent functional identities are present when interactants "mutually impute to self and other sequences of forthcoming behavior" (Scheff, 1970:203). Congruent identities always involve a relationship between the participants and the projection of a shared future. In association, functional identities refer to doing something in relation to another. Functional identities are congruent when they allow for the completion of what interactants recognize as a unit of social activity. Congruent functional identities, then, refer to action taken and projected which set limits to the tone, variability, and intensity of future acts.

Congruent functional identities allow people to project futures with one another where shared foci are transformed into social objectives. When this happens, shared foci become social plans of action to be accomplished through coordinated behavior. Social objectives make social acts possible since, as Mead (1934) argues, all social acts must have achievable ends. Plans of action anticipate endings.

In the case of fanciful recontextualization as a social act of context creation, established congruent functional identities are the opening or beginning of the act. The middle involves the elements of fanciful recontextualization which have been empirically isolated in this research effort, while the ending involves the return to the mundane or ordinary ongoing interaction. Since social foci are integral to social objectives and congruent functional identities (the beginning of the social act of fanciful recontextualization), it is no surprise that the process of fanciful recontextualization depends upon the introduction and transformation of shared foci.

To describe and illustrate the six sequential steps of fanciful recontextualization, four of the eleven fanciful episodes will be discussed in terms of the necessary and ordered features which have been isolated from all of the eleven fanciful episodes.

116

While these four episodes are discussed in a "dissected" form, they appear in their entirety in Figure I, J, K, and L and will be referred to as one of these specific Figures.

Jump Focus

Jump focus, the first sequential element entails the introduction of a fanciful or playful topic. Involved here is a "jump" to a focus different from the immediate one. While the focus that is jumped to introduces a "fanciful" or playful frame to the interaction, the focus nevertheless is <u>related</u> to the ongoing, task-oriented mundane focus of the participants or social actors.

In Figure I the focus jump occurs when Mary exclaims about Anne: "For someone who has MRS on their sweater" [1]. What makes this a jump from the mundane to the fanciful is the irony of the MRS initials on Anne's sweater. The introduction of and jump to "Anne's MRS initials" as the social and shared focus of the interactants provides a new interpretive frame.

In the transcript presented in Figure J when Lois responds: "You don't look sad, you don't have the Eckman and Friesen universal affect display," to Gail's proclamation of: "aw I'm sad," a focus jump occurrences. With her response, Lois introduces a focus which <u>facilitates</u> the "transformation" of Gail's statement from the serious to the playful. An actual transformation is accomplished or completed first, when the fanciful focus has been accepted and second, when it has been elaborated on.

Gail initiates a focus jump in Figure K when she claims to have coded "listens," 3-1-2. "Listens" was a frequent and easy item for coding and without exception had been coded 1-2-3 by the four women. The playfulness manifested or introduced at this point is, in a sense, an occurrence of Hall's (1976) high context episode. In recall, according to Hall's (1976) definition of high context communication ". . . most information is either in the physical context or it is internalized in the person. Very little information is found in the coded, explicit, transmitted part of the message" (Hall, 1976: 91). While in this specific

117

FIGURE I

```
Mary:               For someone with MRS on their sweater
                    (looks at A, then L)     (EC=L)
Gail:

Lois:   All right.
        (looks at papers in front of her) (EC=M)
Anne:
                              (covers MRS with hand)

Mary:           It's embarrassing!

Gail:       MRS?
            (looks at A's sweater)
Lois:   MRS!

Anne:                           My degree I'm after,
                                (points at MRS on her

Mary:

Gail:                   Oh, yeah, right.

Lois:

Anne:   MRS., my MRS. degree.
        sweater)

Mary:

Gail:   What's your fisrt name?  Oh, that's right, we

Lois:   M. S-------- R---! What's M?

Anne:                       Mary.
                            (looks at G)

Mary:                                   That's

Gail:   talked  about that.  From the soap opera.
                    (looks at A)
Lois:                               I forgot
                                    (drinks
Anne:                           soap opera.
```

118

Mary: just what I was thinking.

Gail: Oh, except Mary Ryan's
                                         (looks down at papers)
Lois: about that.
      coffee)
Anne:

Mary:

Gail: dead.

Lois: She's dead (pause) well, um, this says MRS,
           (puts down coffee, looks at A, reaches over
Anne:

Mary: (laughs)

Gail: (laughs)

Lois: what do you think that means? (laughs)
      points at MRS initials)
Anne: (laughs) I'll

Mary: (laughs)

Gail: (laughs)

Lois: (laughs) Okay. We don't

Anne: just get a masters now. (laughs)

Mary:

Gail:

Lois: have to make all of the X's since we did them

Anne:

Mary: the

Gail:

Lois: all together. We just have to read off

Anne:

Mary: numbers, shall I go first?

Gail:

Lois:

Anne:

Mary:

Gail: Aw, I'm sad.

Lois: Well, G, you don't look sad, you
                 (looks at G, sits back in chair,
Anne:

Mary:

Gail:

                          (makes sad
Lois: don't have the E and F universal affect
       shuffles papers, makes face, looks at A, then
Anne:

Mary: What are you suppose to do?
               (makes face at L and A)
Gail:
       face, looks at L)
Lois: display.
       M)
Anne: Don't be sad.
       (looks at G, makes sad face).

Mary:

Gail: Happy!
      (makes face, looks at L and A)
Lois: Startled!   Fear!
      (makes face, positions arms) (makes
Anne: (laughs)   (laughs)
      (looks at M)   (looks at L)

Mary:

Gail:

Lois: I can't get
      fearful face)
Anne: Little round mouth for surprise.
      (looks at G, makes circle with hand)

Mary:

Gail:

Lois: that one. Oh, she's good. Oh, now that's
　　　　　　　(looks at m)
Anne:

Mary:

Gail: 　　　　　　　　　　　　　　　　　　(laughs)
　　　　　　　(makes surprised face)
Lois: coquettish.

Anne: (laughs)　Oh, that's good. You've probably
　　　　　　　(looks at G)

Mary: 　　　　　　　　　　　　　　　　　(laughs)
　　　　　　　　　　　　　　　　　　(hits head with
Gail: 　　　　　　Definitely (laughs) High reliability.

Lois:

Anne: been trained.

Mary: 　　　　　　　　　　　　　　　Is that what you
　　　hand)　　　　　　　　　　　(looks at G)
Gail: I can get it on the non-verbals.

Lois:

Anne:

Mary: teach your students?

Gail: 　　　　　　　　　　Honest.
　　　　　　　(makes serious face)
Lois: 　　　　　　　　　　　　　　Question 7.
　　　(looks at G and then M)
Anne: 　　　　　　　　　　　　Surprise.
　　　(looks at G, makes face)

122

```
Mary:  OHHHH!  1-1-4
Gail:                            3-1-4
Lois:                    3-1-4
Anne:              1-1-4
```

FIGURE K

Mary: Okay, "listens," 1-2-3
        (looks down at papers in front of her)
Gail: 3-2-1
        (looks down at papers in front of her)
Lois: 1-2-3
        (looks down at papers in front of her)
Anne: 1-2-3
        (looks down at papers in front of her)

Mary:
        (leand back in chair, looks at G)
Gail: (laughs)   Sorry (laughing

Lois: What! Are you serious?

Anne:
        (leans back in chair, looks at G)

Mary:

Gail: very hard) I just couldn't resist. It's the
                        (looks down at papers,
Lois:

Anne:

Mary: I was just going to say, it happened. IT

Gail: same.
        shakes head, No)
Lois:

Anne:

Mary: HAPPENED!

Gail: (continues laughing)

Lois: It happened, the dummy
                   (looks down at own papers)
Anne:

Mary: Point to the loon. "Tries to help,"

Gail: (laughs)
               (looks down at own papers)
Lois: emereged. (laughs)

Anne: (laughs)

Mary: 1-2-5

Gail: 1-2-5

Lois: 1-2-5

Anne: 1-2-5

FIGURE L

Mary: (laughs)
                                       (throws head
Gail: (laughs)
                                       (claps hands
Lois: "Lets people make fun of her." (laughs) Yeah!

Anne: A fool!   (laughs)

Mary: (laughs)
        back, looks at A)
Gail: Well, we know it's a woman, right.! (laughs)
        looks at A)
Lois: (laughs)

Anne: (laughs) A

Mary: (laughs) A real Wo-man (laughs)
                     (looks down at own papers)
Gail: (laughs)   Oh
                     (looks down at own papers)
Lois: (laughs)
                     (looks down at own papers)
Anne: true woman. (laughs)
                     (looks down at own papers)

Mary:

Gail: that's also what we're going to include, a

Lois:

Anne:
                (looks up at G)

Mary:

Gail: section in our paper on real women (laughs) in

Lois:

Anne:

126

Mary:

Gail: fact we could write a book: Real Women Let

Lois:

Anne:

Mary: Smile A Lot

Gail: People Make Fun of Them,

Lois: No, real

Anne:

Mary:

Gail:

Lois: women don't smile (laughs) real women don't

Anne:

Mary: (laughs)
          (looks at L)
Gail: (laughs)
          (looks at L)
Lois: listen, real women   (laughs)

Anne: real women are men. (laughs)

Mary: I coded it. . .
                  (looks down at own papers)
Gail:
                  (looks down at own papers)
Lois: Oh dear! "Lets people make fun of her."

Anne:

episode the playful or fanciful context is introduced verbally, its actually playfulness is understandable only to the participants who have a shared past. This shared past constitutes Hall's (1976) "internalized" information. Gail's code 3-1-2 suggests and introduces playfulness since the research group already has an agreed upon and established code for the response in question (listens) and since at an earlier point the participants had joked about someone eventually mis-coding the item. When Gail simultaneously states the code, laughs and shakes her head no, she is clearly stating that this code is the introduction of a playful frame and not a mis-coded item.

In Figure L a focus jump occurs when Anne exclaims: "A Fool!" to the just introduced item: "Lets people make fun of her," for coding. While the introduction of the questionnaire response constitutes part of the ongoing serious interaction, the "definition" of "a fool" begins a transformation of the serious to the fanciful. Anne's statement initiates a playful/fanciful interpretation frame for the immediate forthcoming interaction.

Focus Acceptance

When the new focus (the focus introduced in the "jump focus" stage) has been accepted, when at least one other interactant builds off of the newly introduced focus, then the second ordered and sequential element in the structured process of fanciful recontextualization has been accomplished. In all instances of fanciful recontextualization analyzed here, successful episodes of fanciful recontextualization episodes involved everyone accepting the focus jumped to. With the new focus accepted, the interactants create an agreement to interpret their mutual behaviors and activity from a new interpretation frame. In the case of fanciful recontextualization the new frame is a fanciful one.

The transcript of Figure I shows that Lois and Anne are the first interactants to accept the playful focus introduced by Mary's comment. Lois accepts the focus when she exclaims MRS! while Anne accepts it when she covers the initials on her sweater (MRS) with her hand. Immediately after Lois and Anne accept the focus, Gail does when she asks: MRS?.

Focus acceptance is accomplished in Figure J when first, Gail and Anne make "sad faces" and second, when Mary asks: "What, what are you suppose to do?" All three are choosing to build-off of Lois's fanciful focus of "Eckman and Friesen's universal affect display." Moreover, all three are agreeing not to take Gail's statement: "aw, I'm sad" seriously. They are choosing to recontextualize instead.

Mary is the first of the three interactants to accept the fanciful focus introduced by Gail in Figure K. Immediately after Mary accepts the playful focus, both Lois and Anne simultaneously accept the focus. Lois does so when she asks: "What!? Are you serious?!" and then laughs. By laughing and looking over at Gail, Anne accepts the fanciful focus.

Differing from the other three fanciful episodes discussed, in Figure L Mary, Gail and Lois simultaneously accept the focus jump introduced by Anne. Simultaneous acceptance occurs when all three laugh immediately after Anne's "A Fool!" proclamation. In verbalizing the acceptance of the focus, Lois says "Yeahh!" and then Gail announces; "Well, we know it's a woman."

Elaboration of the Shared Focus

Once the playful focus jump has occured and once it has been built-off of by one other participant, the focus must be elaborated on in order for the third ordered feature of fanciful recontextualization to be completed. The elaboration of the fanciful focus entails all of the participants building on the fanciful topic. Even though this elaboration process involves all of the participants, the messages created may be either verbal or non-verbal or both.

In Figure I Anne elaborates on the now shared focus when she says: "My degree I'm after, MRS, my MRS degree" and simultaneously points at the initials on her sweater. Focus elaboration continues through a discussion of how the MRS initials represent the same name as the one of a popular soap opera character.

Elaboration of the shared focus ends when first Gail notes that in the soap opera that particular character is dead and second when Lois continues: "She's dead (pause) well, um, this says MRS, what do you think that means?" and laughs. While Lois is talking, Anne, at the same time exclaims: "I'LL just get a masters now" and laughs.

Focus elaboration occurs in Figure J when all four members of the research group engage in mimicking emotional "faces" of the Eckman and Friesen universal affect display. On the transcript, elaboration of the shared focus begins with Gail saying "Happy!" and making a "happy face." Focus elaboration ends with Anne making a face and saying "surprise."

The elaboration of the shared focus of Figure K begins with Gail's laughing very hard and saying "Sorry, I just couldn't resist. It's the same." Mary participates in the focus elaboration process when she responds to Gail with: "I was just going to say, it happened, IT HAPPENED!". Lois by saying: "It happened, the dummy emerged" both elaborates on the shared focus and build off of Mary's elaboration of the shared focus. Focus elaboration ends with Mary's statement: "Point to the loon."

Figure L becomes an episode of fanciful recontextualization based on a playful elaboration of what constitutes a "Real Wo-Man." In elaborating on Anne's fanciful focus Mary, while laughing, says: "A real wo-man.". After saying this, Gail, Lois and Anne laugh and continue to elaborate on the fanciful topic. For instance Gail claims: "Oh, that's also what we're going to include, a section in our paper on real women, in fact we could write a book, Real Women Let People Make Fun Of Them". Focus elaboration continues along this theme until Anne says: "Real women are men".

Re-Introduction of The Mundane as Focus

Re-introduction of the mundane focus is the fourth step of the fanciful recontextualization process. Essentially, a request is made by one member that all return to the ongoing mundane task that they had been involved in before the playful interlude began. As in the jump focus stage of the structured process of fanciful recontextualization, this phase need entail only one participant. While one participant is necessary and sufficient, more than one person may be involved in the re-introduction of the mundane as focus.

In Figure I the mundane is re-introduced by Lois. She accomplishes this by saying: "Okay, we don't have to make all of the X's since we did them all together." Lois also re-introduces the mundane as the social focus in both Figure J and L. When Lois states: "Question 7" in Figure J, she re-introduces the mundane. Likewise, in Figure L when she re-states the questionnaire response: "let's people make fun of her," she in re-introducing the mundane. Mary, re-introduces the mundane in Figure K when she states: "Tries to help, 1-2-5." Here, "Tries to help" is the questionnaire response being coded, while 1-2-5 is Mary's code for the response.

The re-introduced mundane focus may either be accepted or not accepted. In Appendix A focus non-acceptance occurs between Fanciful Recontextualization Episodes numbers 1 and 2. I will return to discuss this "non-acceptance loop" at a further point in this chapter.

Re-Introduced Focus Acceptance

In continuing to describe the recontextualization process, the re-introduced mundane focus is accepted when at least one other interactant builds-off of the re-introduced focus. To actually restore the mundane, all of the interactants must accept the re-introduced focus. This sequential step parallels the focus acceptance stage which characterizes the second ordered feature of the structured process of fanciful recontextualization. Once the re-introduced mundane focus has been accepted, then, the interactants have mutually agreed to shift the interpretive frame employed to "make sense" out of each others interaction and messages.

In Figure J, K and L, focus acceptance occurs when an interactant other than the person who re-introduced the mundane, codes the questionnaire item that has been introduced. As a functional equivalent in Figure I,

131

Mary accepts the re-introduced focus when she continues the sentence of Lois's actual re-introduction. The following illustrates.

Mary: the numbers, shall I go

Gail:

Lois: We Just have to read off

Anne:

Mary: first . . .

Gail:

Lois:

Anne:

Ordinary Life Restored

Ordinary life is restored once all of the participants have verbally or nonverbally elaborated on the re-introduced focus. Once the re-introduced focus has been elaborated on then it becomes the shared focus for coordinated activity. In all instances of the fanciful recontextualization data analyzed in this study, ordinary life was restored when the interactants created a "normal" interaction episode.

The Non-Acceptance Loop

When the mundane is re-introduced as a potential shared focus, it may either be accepted or not. If it is not accepted as a shared focus then a return to the fanciful jump focus stage occurrences. In Appendix A episodes number 1 and 2 are an instance of this non-acceptance loop. After the first playful or fanciful episode begins to subside, Lois attempts to re-introduce the mundane. Lois starts to look at the papers in front of her, states: "All right" and then Mary focus jumps to yet another fanciful topic (one different from the one in the first episode).

132

Mary's jump focus interrupts Lois's attempt to return to the mundane task. Once the focus jump has been made, Lois accepts the fanciful topic and the second playful or fanciful episode is underway (the second episode if the one presented in Figure I).

Joking Versus Play

Joking emerged from the data as a natural contrast to successful fanciful recontextualization. I refer to this contrast as joking and not failed play since specific intentionality must be imputed in order to claim something has failed. I claim no knowledge of the operating intentionality involved in the following two "joking" episodes.

In the transcripts of Figure M and Figure N, Lois introduces a fanciful focus jump which in both instances is not elaborated on by any of the other participants. All three other participants, however, accept the focus jumps or at least acknowledge them when they laugh at their introduction. In Figure M the questionnaire response item "reliability" is made fun of by Lois when she immediately exclaims "zero, zero point zero, zero ,zero ,zero," in a mocking voice. Obviously she is commenting about the task that the research team is engaged in---reliability testing. While everyone laughs at her comment,(in other words they get her comment), no one elaborates on it. The lack of elaboration renders the episode one of "joking" versus one of "playing."

Similarly, in the second episode everyone laughs at Lois's: "Boy, someone's going to blow this one time," reference to the frequent and easily coded questionnaire response item, "listens." As has already been documented (see Figure K), "listens" does later become a focus for fanciful recontextualization.

Summary

Six sequential, necessary and ordered features were isolated as the process of fanciful recontextualization. These six characteristics: jump focus, focus acceptance, elaboration of the shared focus, re-introduction of the mundane as shred focus,

"Joking" Episode

Mary: (giggles) "Reliability (laugh)
      (reading from papers, looks at L)
Gail: (laugh)
      (looks at M)   (looks at L)
Lois: (laugh) Zero,zero
      (looks at M)   (mocking voice)
Anne: (laugh)
        (looks at M)   (looks at L)

Mary: (laugh)

Gail: (laugh)

Lois: point zero, zero, zero, zero, (laugh) I
                                              (serious
Anne: (laugh)

Mary:

Gail:

Lois: thought this could mean two very different
      voice)
Anne:

Mary:

Gail:

Lois: things and I had trouble. I would have

Anne:

Mary:

Gail: Uh huh.

Lois: coded it two different ways.   Whether it

Anne:

Mary:

Gail:

Lois: meant someone did things correctly or whether

Anne:

Mary:

Gail: Yeah.

Lois: someone was reliable, interpersonally.

Anne: Yeah.

FIGURE N

"Joking" Episode

Mary:	"Listens," 1-2-3		(laughs)
	(reading from own papers)		(looks up)
Gail:			1-2-3 (laughs)
	(reading from own papers)		(looks up)
Lois:		1-2-3	(laughs)
	(reading from own papers)		(looks up)
Anne:		1-2-3	(laughs)
	(reading from own papers)		(looks up)

Mary:
   (looks at L)
Gail:
   (looks at L)
Lois: Boy, someone's going to blow this one time.
   (looks at M)
Anne:
    (looks at L)

Mary: (laughs) "Eye contact,". . . .
   (reading from own papers)
Gail: (laughs)
   (looking at own papers)
Lois: (laughs)
   (looking at own papers)
Anne: (laughs)
   (looking at aown papers)

acceptance of the mundane as focus, and ordinary life restored have been described in detail. Along with these six elements, a "non-acceptance loop" emerged from the data. While this non-acceptance loop is a possibility in fanciful recontextualization, it is not a necessary and ordered feature of the process.

Social play is closely tied to and made possible by shared foci which "knowingly" or intentionally facilitate transcending the mundane. The transcendence, like the focus, is fanciful. Since social play is intimately related to shared foci, it is the enacting of the elaboration of the shared focus which allows the act to encompass the scene in fanciful recontextualization.

Social play, as previously discussed, allows for the possibility of political play. This possibility is related to the hierarchical conception of fanciful recontextualization which begins with individual play and culminates in political play. The next chapter will elaborate on the notion of political play. In this elaboration the research findings will be discussed within a critical domain.

Endnotes

1.   It is a "preppy" custom to have one's initials embroidered onto sweaters. Customarily a person's last initial is larger than the other two and it is placed in the middle.

C H A P T E R   S I X

Critical Discussion of

Fanciful Recontextualization

The emergence of many political comedians and comedy groups in the last five years marks a new development in the social movements of the sixties and seventies. There is now a radical humor group.. .-(the) Ladies Against Women who claim that telling jokes is more fun than selling newspapers.

If humor is to the eighties what rock music was to the sixties, the Ladies Against Women may be pioneers in the creation of a new kind of political culture" (Escoffier, 1983:5).

Introduction

This final chapter not only discusses the contributions of the study's findings from a critical framework but it also discusses the limitations of the study. Contributions will be dealt with first. As the contributions are discussed a conceptual movement is urged which shifts the focus from fanciful recontextualization to recontextualization.

Contributions

Answering the question: "How are communicative or social contexts created?" contributes to an interpretive understanding of human interaction and behavior. Yet, while my research is guided by an interpretive social science, specifically that of symbolic interaction, the findings are useful in constructing critical social theory.

Critical utility will be established in two ways: first by addressing the parameters of and general links between interpretive and critical social theory, and second, by discussing the connections between the recontextualization process and the process of social change.

Interpretive Theory and Critical Theory Links

Interpretive understandings of human behavior take into account the notions that human actions and human interactivity are "rooted in the self-understandings, perceptions, and intentions of the actors involved. . ." (Fay, 1975:96). Since symbolic interaction theory is built on an interpretive meta-theory, the present research study, as conducted, contributes to interpretive theorizing in general.

Yet as Fay (1975) explains: ". . . a critical social theorist operates in terms of the same assumption as does the interpretive social scientist, namely, that human actions and systems of action are rooted in the self-understandings, perceptions, and intentions of the actors involved, so that it is in terms of these—though not exclusively—that one must understand human action" (p. 96). Habermas (1979), also a critical theorist, concurs.

McCarthy (1978) in an analysis of Habermas', Zur Logik Der Socialwissenschaften, argues that Habermas is attempting to combine interpretive procedures which analyze an actors motivation with a critique of the social structures which may influence these motivations. McCarthy contends:

> As social scientists have long noted, behavior in society depends on the agents' definition of the situation; social actors themselves have an interpretation of their behavior, ideas about what they are doing and why they are doing it. But this definition of the situation, through which the agents' behavioral reactions are mediated, is not simply a matter of subjective motivation, of an

140

> intervening process located inside
> the human organism. The 'meanings'
> to which social action is [sic]
> oriented are primarily
> intersubjective meanings
> constitutive of the social matrix
> in which individuals find
> themselves and act...(McCarthy,
> 1978:146-147).

Habermas, thus, like Fay (1975) argues that an interpretive understanding of an actor's intent is only one step in a sound social scientific approach.

According to both Habermas and Fay, this social scientific procedure of interpretive understanding needs to be coupled with a critique of ideology and social structures which influence action. Moreover, Fay (1975) articulates that "a critical social theory is meant to inform and guide the activities of a class of dissatisfied actors which has been brought into existence by social agencies which it claims can only be comprehended by this theory, and it does so by revealing how the irrationalities of social life which are causing the dissatisfaction can be eliminated by taking some specific action which the theory calls for" (p.98). This view has motivated Habermas (1979) to explore communication because in this area an individual establishes his/her relationship to the external world, to other wo/men and to his/her society.

The contribution, then, of this study to both interpretive and critical social thought is based upon the notion that human nature is not fixed---that actions are historically emergent. To quote Ortega y Gasset: "Man has no nature; only his history." What human beings have, however, is the sophisticated and complex ability to create and use language. As creators and users of symbol systems humans have the constructionary powers to not only breakout of inevitably specific responses to routinized situations but to most importantly create and define the situations which inevitably become routinized.

Arguably, then, communication is constitutive of life since human beings create and define the very situations and contexts within which ongoing conduct takes place and from which meaning is imputed. As

141

Habermas says, one's ability to participate in social interaction can be traced to a universal competence---which he conceives (along with Mead) as a developmental acquisition (see <u>Theorie Des Kommunicative Handlens Sprachpragmatic und Philosophicend Zur Rekonstruktion Des Historischen Materialismus</u>).

Freire (1984) also turns to communication when he observes:

> As we attempt to analyze dialogue as a human phenomenon, we discover something which is the essence of dialogue itself: <u>the</u> word. But the word is more than just an instrument which makes dialogue possible. . . .Within the word we find two dimensions, reflection and action, in such radical interaction that if one is sacrificed--even in part--the other immediately suffers. There is not true word that is not at the same time praxis. Thus to speak a true word is to transform the world (p.75).

Ultimately, in order for critical theory and theorists to accomplish their goals of social science they must "educate" (Fay, 1975; Freire, 1984) social actors to see their worlds from a rhetorical or "theory-laden" perspective. Involved in this education is an attempt by the social scientist to "raise the consciousness" of the actors whose situation s/he is studying (Fay, 1975). In fleshing out what this education process entails, Fay (1975) explains that the "consciousness raising" element involves: "the attempt by the social scientist to provide the means whereby the actor(s) being studied can come to see themselves in ways radically different from their own self-conceptions " (p.108).

Seeing the world in ways radically different from their own self conceptions requires that the social actors in question engage in a process of "recontextualization." Likewise, given the preceding discussion, the recontextualization process is tied to social change. The necessity of understanding how this recontextualization process occurs takes us full circle and returns us to the initial question of this specific research endeavor. It is at this juncture that the connections between recontextualization and social change can be addressed.

Recontextualization and Social Change

The connections between recontextualization and social change as developed here are threefold involving: 1)the relation of micro and macro levels of social life and social analysis, 2)social and public levels of play, and, 3)the application of the research site to public issues.

Micro and Macro Levels of Social Life

The belief that the micro level of ongoing everyday interaction is tied to the macro level of social structure has informed the work of numerous social scientists (cf. Wardell, 1975, 1976; Ropers, 1977; and Habermas, 1970,1971,1973,1975,1978,1979,and 1984). For most of these scholars everyday interaction is synonymous with some conceptualization of communicative action. Ropers (1977) suggests that a Meadian social psychology be merged with a Marxist structural analysis in order to provide a wholistic understanding of human life from both ideationally and materially biased perspectives. Wardell (1976) suggests, along these same lines, that social structure be treated as "always in the process of becoming;" while Franks (1976) argues that Marx's notion of false class consciousness is sufficiently ambiguous that it provides little analytical depth. By adopting some symbolic interaction notions of mind and the evolution of mind, depth is added to the concept making it, if nothing else, researchable.

What Ropers (1977), Wardell (1976) and Franks (1976) all share is an attempt to create or develop a new theory simply by merging and synthesizing already established theoretical concepts. The new theories they strive to create are concerned with establishing connections between social interaction (Wardell, 1976; Ropers, 1977), consciousness (Franks, 1976) and social structure. This early "merger" work, however, remains unsatisfactory in that it stays at a purely theoretical level and does not develop an "emancipatory commitment"

143

as advocated by critical theorists who are concerned with some of these same theoretical issues.

Habermas, however, is exemplar of critical theorists who advocate social science as emancipatory. Habermas (1984) argues that understanding culture and the creation of culture are key to collapsing the false dichotomy of micro and macro levels of social life.

As already mentioned Habermas develops a theory of modern society that places the process of communication in an important role. In developing his argument of communicative action, Habermas (1984) turns to the "paradigm of language" (Habermas, 1984 :ix) in order to understand how ". . .the human species maintains itself through the socially coordinated activities of its members. . ." (p.397). By turning to communication and language Habermas overcomes Marx's (the theorist often credited with being the first critical theorist) ambivalence toward both language and communication. The "paradigm of language" adopted by Habermas is the "ordinary language philosophy" forwarded by Searle (1969) and Austin (1962).

While I agree that language and communication must be addressed in order to collapse the micro/macro dichotomy, I question his choice of ordinary language philosophy. Austin and Searle's analysis is much too narrow to seriously accommodate a notion of social change. Ordinary language philosophy is concerned with convention manifested in patterns of talk. As such meaning is assumed to exist only in the intention of the "speaker" which would---because of convention---be understood by the "hearer" in a conversation.

Mead (1934) provides an alternative notion of meaning. He argues that meaning is in the response to a message. By placing meaning in the response and not in the speakers intention social life is envisioned to have an ephemeral quality not acknowledged by Searle (1969) and Austin (1962). These ephemeral qualities lead to the insistence that everyday social life and social change co-exist.

There are at least two reasons why Habermas and other critical theorists have not relied on a symbolic interactionist interpretive base. By addressing these criticisms I will establish that adopting a symbolic

144

interaction theory as the "interpretive foundation" of critical theory provides a sounder approach to collapsing the micro/macro level distinctions in social life analysis.

Critical theorists have criticized symbolic interaction theory for being both ahistorical as well as for not having institutional level analytical tools. In many ways these objections to symbolic interaction theory are intertwined and contextualized by similar concerns. Symbolic interactionism faces the ahistorical criticism because of the continual insistence on studying the ongoing nature or processual nature of human life. What specifically is being studied is "history in the making." The second criticism is faced for many of the same reasons as "institutions in process" are studied. As I will show these criticisms are also tied to an inadequate notion of social change.

Habermas (1972) has criticized symbolic interaction theory for being ahistorical. For critical theorists the ahistorical criticism is important because through "historical processes" (Marx's dialectical forces of history) institutions evolve and are transformed. Eventually these institutions manifested in historically specific epochs impinge on human beings in particular ways. Moreover, critical theorists argue, these forces explain human behavior. In a nutshell, symbolic interactionists are criticized for not dealing with the grim contingencies of social life.

Couch (1982) offers six different hierarchically arranged "paradigms of thought," presently in existence in social thought. Couch claims that the most complex paradigm is the historical one and that symbolic interaction resides fully in this paradigm. He bases his argument on the consideration of time in symbolic interaction theory (particularly as Mead deals with time). The argument is made that symbolic interaction pays careful theoretical attention to considerations of past, present and the future. Theoretically (see Mead, 1934) it is assumed that the past gives rise to the present while the future causes it. For the historical paradigm, temporality simply isn't the past or a combination of the past enacted in the present, but a consideration of all three. The inclusion of all three dimensions of time allows for a discussion of both persistence and change evolving and being created through time.

A difference exists between the critical school of thought and the symbolic interactionist school regarding the analytical level for approaching the study of history. Analytically critical theorists start at a macro level (eventually, as Habermas does, working their way downward), whereas symbolic interactionists have a micro level starting point.

Symbolic interaction theory, to elaborate, posits that relationships and people creating social units over time have histories as people co-create meanings, reify meanings and change meanings by mutually communicating and impinging on one another. Relationships, as they become patterned, create social structures. Because of the "force of history" (dialectical force or otherwise), through habituation, relationships become impinging. Interacting humans, however, may breakout of any impingements.

For symbolic interaction theory the image of the relationship of human beings to society, thus, starts with a focus on interacting humans actively creating a history. A macro level starting point to the analysis of social life begins with the assumption that society exists in a sui generis (having a life of its own) manner. Hence, structural forces are tied to the force of history as historically established structures make people act in specified ways. Symbolic interaction theory envisions humans as much more active and as such begins with the premise of interactivity. Interactivity, then, presumes that language and the concept of a future allows for change.

Contextual change or structural change does not simply happen because time marches on. Social structures and social contexts are created through social interaction (and mutual definitions of situations) as it is constructed over time. Human beings are able to interact because they create and use language (significant symbols). Persons are also able to project futures because they use language. Since people are able to project futures (by rehearsing possible future bounded episodes through an internalized conversation of gestures) they are able to engage in directed intentional change (based on a vision of what a future would look like).

Interacting humans, thus, are responsible for the construction of social contexts (through joint behavior and interpersonal communication) and social structures as well as changes in these (intentional or otherwise) occuring over time.

Along with the ahistorical criticism, symbolic interaction theory has also been criticized for not having tools for institutional analysis.

As a critical theorist Habermas claims that interaction is shaped by institutional contexts and these institutions entail contradictions thereby preventing certain definitions of reality. The claim becomes that since symbolic interaction doesn't have the analytical tools for studying institutions then the theory cannot provide an adequate explanation of the action observed.

Assumption differences between symbolic interaction theory and critical theory account for this criticism. Critical theorists (Habermas, 1984; Fay, 1978) assume that institutions are harboring contradictions and as such force people to act in particular ways as well as to prevent them from discovering the existent institutional contradictions. While symbolic interactionists may be sympathetic to the claim that institutional contradictions exist, they do not assume the truthful existence of institutional contradictions. This stems, in part, from a methodological commitment.

Methodologically symbolic interactionists adhere to an inductive research protocol. This protocol stands in the way of assuming institutional contradictions but not in the way of "discovering" them. Arguably, then, the analytical tools of symbolic interaction by no means prevent the analysis of institutions. Again, institutions are social structures which are simply made-up of a web of patterned interaction. As Mead (1934) contends institutions come into being and continue to exist through common definitions.

Whatever else institutions are, they are humanly and actively created. Since interactionists are interested in making sense out of patterned interaction and since it is that which they study, institutions and the contradictions manifested in them are all possible foci for analysis. In fact, institutional level activity has been the focus of a number of classical symbolic interactionist studies. Rose in the late 1940's studied unions and union activity just as Blumer (1947) studied the fashion industry. Since 1964 Anselm Strauss has been involved in a continual series of studies which focus attention on hospital contexts. Whyte conducted an institutional analysis of restaurants during the 1950's while Denzin (1976) and Faberman (1975) respectively conducted similar studies on the liquor industry and used automobile industries. All of the studies cited describe institutional contradictions and structures as they are manifested in patterns of social interaction.

By analyzing patterned interaction researchers are able to detect structuring and relationships not detectable by the human actors involved. Contradictions, thus, are detectable or discoverable (as in both Denzin's work and Faberman's work) but these contradictions are not assumed a priori.

To recap, two of the major criticisms of symbolic interaction theory made by critical theorists (Habermas among them) have been refuted. Refutation helps to establish that symbolic interaction theory can provide an interpretive base for critical theory---particularly as Habermas conceives critical theory. Symbolic interaction theory facilitates Habermas's commitment to collapsing micro and macro levels of analysis. Facilitating this commitment is the theory's conceptualization of interactivity which encompasses communication, social activity or behavior, temporally emergent relationships, and social structuring in terms of the patterned web of established relationships.

As an interpretive theory symbolic interaction does not have a stated commitment to either emancipatory research questions and protocols or the application of research to public issues (although in all fairness Becker's article "Whose Side Are We On" begins to address possible applications of research). For critical theorizing the public sphere is an essential consideration. According to Habermas (1974) the public sphere is: ". . .first of all a realm of our social life in which something approaching public opinion can be found. Access is guaranteed to all citizens. A portion of the public sphere comes into being in every conversation in which private individuals assemble to form a public body" (p.49).

For my research the connections between social fanciful recontextualization and public fanciful recontextualization embrace Habermas's commitment to emancipatory social science by applying the research model to public issues. In order to discuss the application of the model, the connections between social and public fanciful recontextualization will be made. This connection relies on the data generated from this research endeavor.

Levels of Play
        Earlier I argued that there are three hierarchical levels of analysis within which human play may be studied. While this hierarchy has already been introduced, a re-introduction is in order for this discussion. This hierarchical discussion illustrates the utility of understanding fanciful recontextualization to a critical perspective by setting a framework for applying the research to public issues.

        Individual play, social play, and public play form the fanciful recontextualization hierarchy. While the hierarchy implies that each level is dependent upon the previous one, what differentiates each of these levels from one another are the consequences of the activity. As claimed in chapter three, the distinctions identified between each level of play are heuristic.

        Briefly, individual play is largely a cognitive activity where individuals fancifully imagine possible overt activity. The consequences of this type of fanciful recontextualization are internal to the individual, e.g. titillation, easing discomfort, etc.

        Social play has the social function of creating solidarity among equals or among unequals who have the real possibility of becoming equals in the future. As such social play does not alter existing relationships. Nevertheless while engaging in social play the participants can make comments on their relationships with one another as well as collective relationships to other social phenomena. Essentially. the consequences of this type of play are the creation of cohesion among the participants and the reification of the participants social relationships to one another.

Likewise, in facilitating the formulation of shared definitions of "larger" relationship issues regarding perceived generalized others, e.g. a generalized view of the societal position of women, social play provides the foundation for public fanciful recontextualization. For instance, in the following two transcripts (Figures O and P) from the data Mary, Gail, Lois, and Anne playfully comment on perceptions of women.

The topics of these transcripts of fanciful recontextualization may be built upon in a public manner, resulting in very different consequences for the activity. Indeed, the example of Ladies Against Women---to be discussed in the next section---is exemplar of this. Hence what social play provides, in this hierarchical model of play, is a starting point for developing and sharing ideas and perceptions that may be translated into public issues and conceptualizations. Social play may be thought of as the starting point for consciousness raising which is necessary for engaging in public play. This can also be a private form of expressing an already raised consciousness.

Public play, then, has the consequence of making comments on existing social relationships (afterall, public play is dependent and built upon social play) as well as the consequence of altering authoritarian relationships which <u>social actors find repressive</u>. The next section, discussing the application of the research site to public settings and issues, further illustrates public play.

Application of Model to Public Settings:
Born to Clean, Born to Clean
In chapters one and three examples and brief analyses of public play were presented. Ladies Against

150

Social Play Transcript

Mary: If you look at the list of all of the bad or
(looks down at papers)

Gail:
(looks down at papers)

Lois:
(looks down at papers)

Anne:
(looks down at papers)

Mary: negative characteristics are coded female.

Gail: Yeah,
                                                    (serious

Lois:

Anne:

Mary: .

Gail: women are sorry creatures who lack skills but
sounding voice, looks at L, EC=L)

Lois:
                                        (EC=G)

Anne:

Mary: (laughs) That's what it sounds
                                 (leans back in chair,

Gail: who give of themselves (laughs)
                                 (looks at M)

Lois: (laughs)

Anne: (laughs)

Mary: like you. . .
looks at G and then L)

Gail:

Lois: Women are (pause) we'll write it,
                                 (looks at m)

Anne:
(looks down at own papers)

Mary: That

Gail:

Lois: this in our paper. Women are sorry creatures

Anne:

Mary: should be the first line in the introduction
        (continues looking at L)
Gail:

Lois:

Anne:

Mary: (laughs)

Gail:

Lois:

Anne: (laughs) Women are (pause) and we have evidence

Mary: This is
                                               (looks
Gail:

Lois: (laughs) Yes we can prove that.
                                  (looks down at own papers)
Anne: to prove it (laughs)

Mary: research done by women, so, of course, sexism
        down at own papers)
Gail:

Lois:

Anne:

```
Mary:  can't be an issue

Gail:              be an issue, right, sexist? me?
                   (looks down at own papers)
Lois:

Anne:


Mary:  Women aren't sexist (laughs) right.

Gail:                    (laughs)

Lois:                    (laughs)

Anne:                    (laughs)  Uhh, okay, so
                                   (looks down at

Mary:

Gail:

Lois:

Anne:  we had done. . .
       own papers)
```

FIGURE P

Social Play Transcript

Mary: (laughs)
                                         (throws head
Gail: .   (laughs)
                                         (claps hands
Lois: "Lets people make fun of her." (laughs) Yeah!

Anne: A fool!   (laughs)

Mary: (laughs)
         back, looks at A)
Gail: Well, we know it's a woman, right.! (laughs)
         looks at A)
Lois: (laughs)

Anne: (laughs) A

Mary: (laughs) A real Wo-man (laughs)
                          (looks down at own papers)
Gail: (laughs)   Oh
                          (looks down at own papers)
Lois: (laughs)
                          (looks down at own papers)
Anne: true woman. (laughs)
                          (looks down at own papers)

Mary:

Gail: that's also what we're going to include, a

Lois:

Anne:
                 (looks up at G)

154

Mary:

Gail: section in our paper on real women (laughs) in

Lois:

Anne:

Mary:

Gail: fact we could write a book: Real Women Let

Lois:

Anne:

Mary: Smile A Lot

Gail: People Make Fun of Them,

Lois: No, real

Anne:

Mary:

Gail:

Lois: women don't smile (laughs) real women don't

Anne:

Mary: (laughs)
       (looks at L)
Gail: (laughs)
        (looks at L)
Lois: listen, real women   (laughs)

Anne: real women are men. (laughs)

Mary: I coded it. . .
          (looks down at own papers)
Gail:
          (looks down at own papers)
Lois: Oh dear! "Lets people make fun of her."

Anne:

Women were discussed in the first chapter while
Patric McMurphy's attempt to fancifully recontextualize
the tyrannically authoritarian relationships he and
Nurse Rachett were engaged in was discussed in the
third chapter. Following is a third instance of public
play. It along with the other two provide concrete
examples of 'critical street theorizing' (I do not use
this term in a derogatory sense).

Mrs. T. Bill (Edith) Banks and Mrs. Chester
(Virginia) Cholesterol, members of the San Francisco
Bay Area Ladies Against Women chapter, when interviewed
by the Socialist Review allow the overall interview
(two parts) itself to emerge as the initial scene.
Consider the following from the first half of the
interview:

SR: Let me ask you a question that we at Socialist
Review are interested in asking.

EDITH BANKS: Oh my goodness!

VIRGINIA CHOLESTEROL: This is Socialist Review?
What have we done? I thought it was Socializing
Review!

EDITH BANKS: I thought it was the Social Register!
(p.13).

The second half of the interview, then, consists of a
"serious" interview with Gail Williams (Virginia
Cholesterol) and Selma Vincent (Edith Banks), who
comment on their activities as LAW members.

SR: What do you see as the role of humor on the
left?

WILLIAMS: What I feel best about in doing comedy
and satire is that it can really bring a lot of
people together, and give you a sense that there is
a critical community that doesn't like what's going
on. . .

VINCENT: We primarily see ourselves as doing
educational work (p.20).

157

Within the initial scene of the overall interview the LAW members purposefully act to name their worldview into existence; LAW members are not <u>women</u>, they are <u>ladies</u>. The "purposeness" of the act creates a tension with the scene, eventually allowing the act to contain the scene. Humor is their agency.

SR: I think I would like to start out by asking a rather basic question, and that is: What do you see as the role of women in politics?

EDITH BANKS: That's exactly the problem, we don't believe that anyone should be women at all; our organization is Ladies <u>Against</u> Women. We believe that ladies should be ladies; no one should be women, especially men. . . .

SR: Let me rephrase the question: What is the role of Ladies in politics?

VIRGINIA CHOLESTEROL: Preparing coffee cake, standing beside successful husband candidates on election night, giving fundraisers, and bake sales.

Not only are LAW members <u>ladies</u>, but they are ladies with a philosophy on life.

SR: According to your organization when do you believe that life begins?

VIRGINIA CHOLESTERAL: At marriage as far as I'm concerned.

The ways in which the agents (LAW members) organize their behaviors are the act in the episode. LAW members <u>act</u> for both themselves and an audience. In the second half of the interview the following takes place:

SR: When Ladies Against Women performs, it seems you are assuming that you're dealing with a generally sophisticated, somewhat feminist audience that will understand you satirizing the right. How are you educating people in this situation?

VINCENT: I know that there are parts in my personal life that are very advanced, and there are parts of

158

my life that are very reactionary, very traditional. By pushing things to the extreme and bringing so many aspects in, we are having women look at the totality of their lives and maybe seeing certain areas and saying: "Wow! I'm as bad as Virginia Cholesterol, maybe I should take a look when I go home tonight."... I think it helps to keep the edge on people's commitment to change, to take the other side and exaggerate it so badly that they see the absurdity of the hypocrisy in their own lives. . . .

LAW intentionally/purposefully act in chosen scenes in order to comment on the existing social order. LAW member Gail Williams (Virginia Cholesterol) names their acts: "performances in the streets" (p.22). In describing one such performance Mrs. Cholesterol states:

> Some of those Republicans are very tasteful people, but I think there are actually some of them who come perilously close to being liberals. I have no idea what they're doing in the Republican Party, but there are all kinds of people who make all kinds of compromises. We found that when we went to the Republican convention in 1980 in beautiful downtown Detroit, that while we were walking around with our little picket signs, many of the Republican delegates were actually embarrassed by our presence and didn't want to speak to us. We stood there with our signs that said "Off the Poor" and "Make America a Man Again," and so forth, and we called out to those Republicans and said "Come out of your closets, stand up for what you believe in," and they would scurry away (p.13).

Purposefulness is also, for LAW, tied to recontextualization (fanciful recontextualization, in particular). For instance, when they argue to "Uphold the paternity rights of men who choose rape or incest as a means of perpetuating their family lineage" (p.22)

159

they do not expect to be taken seriously in the actual contexts of <u>raping</u> and <u>incesting</u>. When they chant: "Hit us again, hit us again, harder, harder," they don't expect husbands to go home and beat their wives. LAW expect laughter, which indicates an understanding the rape, incest, and wife beating are not only "bad" but possible because of a paternalistic--male oriented/controlled--social structure. However, consider the following exchange:

SR: Certain jokes seem to go over in certain circles and not in others, and there's not much logic to it. You might tell a radical joke among a third-world audience and they'll laugh and then a white audience won't or a joke that will go over with gays and lesbians but not in a straight crowd. What do you think the dynamic is in these situations?

WILLIAMS: It's a real hard thing to tell because I think that within the context of what we're doing, we're also advocating total nuclear annihilation and a lot of other things that make it clear what our perspective is. Nevertheless, people that listen to us imagine someone taking it out of context, and even though they think it's funny at the time, they object because they feel someone in the audience will take it seriously.

So not only do LAW members "fancifully recontextualize"--they must do so effectively/obviously enough to ensure that their fancifully recontextualized <u>acts</u> are not themselves recontexted.

SR: What makes one audience laugh and not another? Why might some radical jokes go over in a third world audience and not in a white one?

WILLIAMS: I think that one of the things that people have to be clear about is in a group that's going to laugh together, you have to trust that everyone knows what is true and not true, and that you're all laughing for the same reasons. Then you're comfortable. But if you think that some of them are laughing because they truely are racist, then you don't want to laugh.

160

When Ladies Against Women perform they initiate a jump focus from the mundane. For instance, by appearing at the Republican National Convention in Detroit the comedy troupe presents a focus alternative from the serious convention activities. Once LAW are attended to by persons outside of the group, then, an audience is created. This creation of an audience shifts the recontextualization process from a social setting to a public one. Moreover, once an audience (of at least one person) is created then focus acceptance has occured. As the LAW members continue to enact their "routines" (I use this term loosely) with an audience, the fanciful focus is elaborated on. The mundane focus is re-established when LAW members return to their "just ordinary folks" stance. In other words, when the members of Ladies Against Women stop preforming then the mundane is re-introduced. Once this focus has been accepted (after all demands for encores have stopped or been satisfied) ordinary life is restored.

To summarize, public play is both a rhetorical act and a political activity. As I argue it, the public fanciful recontextualization of ongoing serious activity presents a challenge to an opposing, "oppressive" group in such a manner as to attempt to persuade a permanent alternative. In the act of "persuasion" a temporary alternative is praxically enacted. Throughout this book three episodes of public/political play have been presented and analyzed.

What Patric McMurphy and the Ladies against Women understand, first and foremost is that meaning is in the response. While we all live in world's over which we do not have total control--afterall, there are some grim contingencies to social life--we can "control" our responses in certain situations. Controlling responses is part of the "social game" of everyday life. These controlled responses, in part, create the meaning of the situations being responded to. Patric McMurphy knows ultimately that his playing--his comments--are not going to change the power structure of the insane asylum permanently. Whatever the price, he is able to "equalize" the power differentials for as long as the "playing is prolonged. McMurphy's behavior is the living of Duncan's observation: ". . . through the help of the social game people actually play society" (Duncan, 1967:25).

The Ladies Against Women, also living out Duncan's dictum, "equalize" power differentials by "playing" at being the "power structure." What the members of Ladies Against Women show us, then, is that power structures are people acting and creating. If people act and create differently then different structures will emerge. So while advocating different choices for behavior---they choose to play.

Public fanciful recontextualization allows for: 1) education, 2) consciousness raising, and 3) direct contact with the praxicality of everyday interaction. It is only able to do so because people have engaged in social play---because people know how to fancifullly recontextualize their behaviors. By knowing how fanciful recontextualization takes place, critical social scientists may use this activity to critically inform social actors of how social structures work as well as how social actors make the social structures work. Further, by recontextualizing or by engaging in this process, social actors are given a peek (if nothing else) at how to re-work social ordering.

Some Final Notes: Limitations of the Study and Suggestions for Future Research

The limitations of this study are twofold. First, the study is limited because it is a case study. As a case study generalizability to other groups is limited. This limitation makes it difficult to assess whether or not the findings are unique to the observed behaviors of the single group studied. Of course, two justifications support the original choice of employing a case study analysis. This work is exploratory. As mentioned in earlier chapters few social scientists have empirically and systematically studied the social construction of context. Regardless of this paucity of research, most social theory relies on the assumption that all findings are contextually bound.

Moreover, while a case study analysis was employed the unit of analysis was operationalized as instances of fanciful recontextualization. Operationalizing the unit of analysis in this manner transformed the number of observances from the number of groups observed to the number of episodes of fanciful recontextualization emergent in the groups behavior.

The second limitation of this study is found in the generated model of fanciful recontextualization (see p.159). As formulated, the model appears to be a "closed system." While this model was generated from the observed data it provides a "point in time" picture of the fanciful recontextualization process. Unfortunately, this point in time snapshot can mistakenly be interpreted to be a mechanistic model. In a sense, the model depicts three things---an initial context shift in terms of a focus jump and focus acceptance, sustaining the context shift in terms of focus elaboration, and a context shift back to the mundane. Futhermore, the developed model cannot accommodate unsuccessful or failed attempts to recontextualize the mundane.

Future research should be geared toward overcoming these limitations. To that end, I envision two avenues for research.

First, an attempt to study the process of recontextualization of more groups whose tasks are dissimilar to one another should be made. By studying a number of diversified groups, using the findings from the present research as sensitizing concepts, will reveal if indeed the findings from this analysis are idiosyncratic or unique. Also, an analysis of the recontextualization process of diversified groups will allow for theoretical refinements regarding the specification of the formal properties of context creation. To allow for theoretical refinement a research site other than play should be developed to study recontextualization.

Second, an attempt must be made to research instances of failed recontextualization. Since a researcher doing ethnographic and naturalistic research always runs the risk of not generating data pertinent to a specific question---quasi-experimental research regarding unsuccessful recontextualization should be conducted. As a quasi-experimental technique breaching experiments could be conducted. Studying failed recontextualization will facilitate broadening the "point in time" processual model formulated from this research project.

SELECTED BIBLIOGRAPHY

Abrahams, R.
1976   Talking Black. Rowley, Ma.: Newbury
               Publishing House.

Aldis, O.
1975   Play Fighting. New York: Academic Books.

Aune, J.
1979   "The Contribution of Habermas to Rhetorical
           Validity" Journal of the American Forensic
           Association, vol. 16, Fall.

Bales, R.F.
1970   Personality and Interpersonal Behavior.
           New York: Holt, Rhinehart and Winston.

Barnlund, D.C.
1981   "Toward an Ecology of Communication." in
           Carol Wilder-Mott (ed.) Rigor and
           Imagination: Essays From The Legacy of
           Gregory Bateson. New York: Praeger
           Publishers.

Bateson, G.
1972   Steps to an Ecology of Mind. New York:
           Ballentine.

Becker, H.
1967   "Whose Side are we On?" Social Problems,
           14:239-248.

Beckoff, M.
1975   "The Communication of Play Intention: Are
           Play Signals Functional?" Semiotica,
           15, #3: 231-239.

Berger, P.
1969   A Rumour of Angles: Modern Society and the
           Discovery of the Supernatural. New York:
           Double Day.

Berger, P. and Luckman, T.
1967   The Social Construction of Reality. Garden
           City: Double Day

Bernstein, R.
1978   The Restructuring of Social and Political
           Theory. Philadelphia: University of
           Pennsylvania Press.

Bettleheim, B.
1977   The Uses of Enchantment: The Meaning and
           Importance of Fairy Tales.   New   York:
           Vintage Books.

Birdwhistle, R.
1970   Kinesics   and   Context.   Philadelphia:
           University of Pennsylvania Press.

Blumer, H.
1955   "What's Wrong with Sociological Theory?"
           American Sociological Review, 19: 3-10.

1969   Symbolic Interaction. Englewood Cliffs,
           New Jersey: Prentice Hall.

1972a   "Society as Symbolic Interaction." in Manis
           and Meltzer (eds.), Symbolic
           Interactionism: A Reader in Social
           Psychology. Boston: Allyn and Beacon, Inc.

1972b   "Sociological Analysis and the Variable,"
           in Manis and Meltzer (eds.), Symbolic
           Interactionism: A Reader in Social
           Psychology. Boston: Allyn and Beacon.

Bogdan and Taylor
1975   Introduction to Qualitative Methods.
           New York: John Wiley and Sons.

Bolough, R.
1976   "On Fooling Around: A Phenomenological
           Analysis of PLayfulness." The Annals of
           Phenomenological Sociology, 1: 113-125.

Borgatta and Bohrnstedt
1974   "Some Limitations on Generalizability
           from Social Psychological Studies."
           Sociological Methods and Research, #3:
           111-120.

Borman, E.
1975   Discussion and Group Method: Theory and
Practice. 2nd. Edition. New York:
Harper and Row.

Branham and Pearce.
1985   "Between Text and Context: Toward a
Rhetoric of Contextual Reconstruction." The
Quarterly Journal of Speech, Vol.71:
February.

Brown, R.
1974   A Poetic For Sociology. Cambridge:
Cambridge University Press.

Buban, S.
1979   "Symbolic Interactionism and the Study
of Social Process: The Iowa and
Chicago Schools Revisited." Paper
Presented to the SSSI meetings.

Burke, K.
1945   A Grammar of Motives. New York:
Prentice Hall.

1969   A Rhetoric of Motives. Berkley: University
of California Press.

Burleson, B.
1979   "On The Foundation of Rationality: Toulmin,
Habermas, and the A Priori of Reason"
Journal of the American Forensic
Association, vol. 16, Fall.

Callios, R.
1961   Men, PLay and Games. New York: The Free
Press.

Caplan, F.
1974   The Power of Play. Garden City: Anchor
Press.

Cicorel, A.
1964   Method and Measurement in Sociology.
New York: The Free Press.

Combs, J.
1982   "The Study of Popular Culture and the
            Theory of Play." Paper presented to
            The International Communication
            Conference at Boston.

Cottrel, L.
1950   "Some Neglected Problems in Social
            Psychology." American Sociological Review,
            15: 705-712.

Couch, C.J.
1970   "Some Dimensions of Association in
            Collective Behavior Episodes." Sociometry,
            33: 457-471.

1977a   "The Use of Videotape Recordings in the
            Study of Social Processes." Paper
            presented to the National Meetings of
            The American Sociological Association.

1977b   "Why Methodologists Inhibit the Study
            of Social Behavior." University of
            Iowa, unpublished manuscript.

1978   "Paradigms of Thought." University of
            Iowa, unpublished manuscript.

1979   "Generating Data to Establish Sociological
            Principles." Paper presented to the SSSI
            Meetings.

Couch, C. and Hintz, R. (eds.)
1975   Constructing   Social Life.   Champaign:
            Stipes.

Cronen, V. and Davis, L.
1978   "Alternative Approaches for the
            Communication Theorists: Problems in the
            Laws-Rules-Systems Trichotomy." Human
            Communication Research, 2: 120-128.

Cronen, V. and Lannamann, J.
1981   "This is not the Title: A Theoretical
            and Empirical Approach to Reflexivity
            in Systems of Social Meaning." Paper
            presented to the International
            Communication Association conference.

Csikzentmihalyi, M.
1975   Beyond Boredom and Anxiety. San Fransisco:
        Jossey-Boss Publishers.

Cushman and Dietrich
1979   "A Critical Reconstruction of Jurgen
        Habermas'Holistic Approach to Rhetoric as
        Social Philosophy" Journal of the American
        Forensic Association, vol. 16, Fall.

Denzin, N.
1970   The Research Act. Chicago: Aldine
        Publisher Company.

1975   "Play, Games and Interaction: The Contexts
        of Childhood Socialization." Sociological
        Quarterly, 16: 458-478.

Douglas, J.
1970a   The Relevance of Sociology. New York:
        Appleton-Century Crofts.

1970b   Deviance and Respectability: The Social
        Construction of Moral Meanings. New York:
        Basic Books.

1970c   Understanding Everyday Life. Chicago:
        Aldine Publishing Company.

Dreitzel, P. (ed.)
1970   Recent Sociology, No. 2: Patterns of
        Communication Behavior. New York: The
        MacMillian Company.

Duncan, H.
1962   Communication and the Social Order. New
        York: Oxford University Press.

Ehrann, J.
1971   Games and PLay Literature. Boston:
        Beacon Press.

Ellis, M.
1973   Why People PLay. Englewood Cliffs, N.J.:
        Prentice Hall.

Erikson, E.
1937   "Configurations in Play." Psychoanalytic
          Quarterly, 6: 45-50.

Farrel, T.
1979   "Habermas on Argumentation Theory: Some
            Emerging Topics" Journal of the American
            Forensic Association, vol. 16, Fall.

Fay, B.
1975   Social Theory and Political Practice.
          London: George, Allen and Unwin.

Fine, M.; Johnson, F.L.; Ryan, M.S.; and
Lutfiyya, M.N.
1986   "Ethical Issues Emerging From The
          Evaluation of Women's Communication."
          Communication, Gender and Sex Roles in
          Diverse Interaction Contexts, L.P. Stewart
          and S. Ting-Toomey (eds). Norwood, N.J.:
          Ablex Publishing Company.

Freire, P.
1984   Pedagogy of the Oppressed. New York:
          Continuum Books.
Frank, L.
1955   "Play in Personality and Development."
          American Journal of Orthopsychiatry, 25.

Freud, S.
          Beyond The Pleasure Principle. London:
          Hogarth Press.

Gadamer, H.
1975   Truth and Method. London: Sheed and Ward.

Garfinkle, H.
1967   Studies in Ethnomethodology. New York:
          Prentice Hall.

Garvey, C.
1970   Play. Cambridge, Ma.: Harvard University
          Press.

Geertz, C.
1974   The Interpretation of Culture. New York:
          Harper and Row.

Giddens, A.
1977   Studies in Social and Political Theory.
            New York: Basic Books.

Giglioli, P.
1972   Language and Social Context. New York:
            Penguin.

Glasser, T.
1982   "Play, Pleasure and the Value of
            Newsreading." Communications Quarterly, 30:
            101-107.

Glasser, B. and Strauss, A.
1964   "Awareness Contexts and Social
            Interaction." American Sociological Review,
            29: 669-679.

1967   The Discovery of Grounded Theory:
            Strategies for Qualitative Research.
            Chicago: Aldine Publishing Company.

Goffman, I.
1955   "On Face Work." Psychiatry, 18: 213-231.

1963   Behavior in Public Places. New York:
            The Free Press.

1974   Frame Analysis. New York: Harper and Row.

Gonos, G.
1977   " 'Situation' versus 'Frame:'Interactionist
            and Structuralist Analysis of Everyday
            Life." American Sociological Review, 42:
            854-867.

Gouldner, A.
1970   The Coming Crisis in Western Sociology.
            New York: Basic Books.

1976   The Dialectic of Ideology and Technology.
            New York: The Seabury Press.

Grimshaw, A.
1980   "Social Interactional and Socio-linguistic
            Rules." Social Forces, 58: 789-810.

Gross, K
    1901   The Play of Man. New York: Appleton and
                Company.

Gulick, L.
    1920   A Philosophy of Play. New York:
                Scribneis and Sons.

Habermas, J.
    1970   Zur Logik der Sozialwissenschafen.
                Frankfort: Suhr Kamp.

    1970   Toward a Rational Society. Boston: Beacon
                Press.

    1971   Knowledge and Human Interests. Boston:
                Beacon Press.

    1973   Theory and Practice. Boston: Beacon Press.

    1974   "The Public Sphere" in The New German
                Critique, 1, p. 49.

    1975   Legitimation Crisis. Boston: Beacon Press.

    1979   Communication and the Evolution of Society.
                Boston: Beacon Press.

    1984   The Theory of Communicative Action.
                Boston: Beacon Press.

Handelman, D.
    1974   "A Note on Play." American Anthropologist,
                76: 66-68.

Heider, K.
    1975   Ethnographic Film. Austin: University of
                Texas Press.

Held, D.
    1980   Introduction To Critical Theory. Berkley:
                University of California Press.

Henricks, T.
    1983   "Ascending and Descending Meaning: A
                Theoretical Inquiry in Play and Ritual."
                Sociological Inquiry, 50: 25-37.

Hewitt, J. and Stokes, R.
1973   "Disclaimers." American Sociological
             Review, 40: 1-11.

Hoffman, A.
1968   Revolution for the Hell of it. New York:
          Pocket Books.

Huizinga, J.
1955   Homo Ludens. Boston: Beacon Press.

Johnson, F.L.
1983   "Political and Pedagogical Implications of
          Attitudes Towards Women's Language."
          Communication Quarterly, 31: 133-138.

Johnson, F.L.; Fine, M.; Lutfiyya, M.N.; and Ryan, M.S,
1983   "Working Women's Perception's of
          Communication." Paper presented to the
          Speech Communication Association Annual
          Meetings, Washington, D.C..

Kesey, K.
1962   One Flew Over the Cuckoo's Nest. New York:
          Signet Books.

Kline, S.
1979   "Toward a Contemporary Linguistic
          Interpretation of the Concept of Stasis"
          Journal of The American Forensic
          Association, vol. 16, Fall.

Kochman, T.
1981   Black and White Styles in Conflict.
          Chicago: University of Chicago Press.

Kramarae, C.
1983   Women and Men Speaking. Rowley, MA.:
          Newberry House Publishing.

Krippendorf, K.
1980   Content Analysis: An Introduction to its
          Methodology.   Beverly Hills: Sage
          Publications.

Kuhn, M.
1964   "Major Trends in Symbolic Interaction
            Theory in the Past Twenty-five Years."
            Sociological Quarterly, 5: 61-84.

Kuhn, T.
1962   The Structure of Scientific Revolutions.
            Chicago: University of Chicago Press.

Labov, W.
1972   "Rules for Ritualized Insults." in
            D. Sudnow (ed.). Studies in Social
            Interaction.

Labov and Fanshell
1977   Therapeutic Discourse. New York:
            Academic Press.

Levy, J.
1978   Play Behavior. New York: Wiley.

Lofland, J.
1970   "Intercationist Imagery and Analytic
            Interruptus."in T. Shibutani (ed.).
            Human Nature and Collective Behavior.
            Englewood Cliffs, N.J.: Prentice Hall.

1971   Analyzing Social Settings.Belmot, Ca.:
            Wadsworth Publishing Company, Inc. .

Lutfiyya, M. N.
1980   The Social Process of Interpersonal
            Accounting. Unpublished M.A. Thesis,
            University of Iowa.

Lutfiyya, M. N. and Miller, D.
1986   "Disjunctures and the Process of
            Interpersonal Accounting." in Couch,
            Saxton, and Katovich (eds.) Studies in
            Symbolic Interaction, Volume 6. Greenwich,
            Conn.: JAI Press.

Lyman and Scott
1967   "Territoriality: A Neglected Sociological
            Dimension." Social Problems, 15: 236-249.

Maines, D.
1977   "Social Organization and Social Structure
in Symbolic Interactionist Thought."
Annual Review of Sociology, 3: 235-259.

Maines, D., Sugrue, N., and Katovich, M.
1983   "The Sociological Import of G.H. Mead's
Theory of the Past." American Sociological
Review, 48: 161-173.

Malinowski, B.
1923   "The Context of Situation." in Ogden and
Richards (eds.). The Meaning of Meaning.
New York: Harcourt, Brace and World, Inc. .

Markley, D.
1980   Psychological Development and Problems of
Readjustment Among Vietnam Veterans.
Unpublished M.A. thesis, Cleveland State
University, Cleveland Ohio.

McCarthy, T.
1978   The Crtical Theory of Jurgen Habermas.
Cambridge MA.: MIT Press.

Mead, G. H.
1934   Mind, Self and Society. Chicago:
University of Chicago Press.

1938   Philosophy of the Act. Chicago: University
of Chicago Press.

1956a   On Social Psychology. Chicago: University
of Chicago Press.

1956b   Movements of Thought in the Nineteenth
Century. Chicago: University of
Chicago Press.

1964   "The Nature of the Aesthetic Experience."
in A. J. Peck (ed.). The Selected
Writings of G. H. Mead. Indianapolis:
Bobbs-Merrill.

Meltzer and Petras
1970   "The Chicago and Iowa Schools of Symbolic
Interaction." In Manis and Meltzer (eds.).

Milgram, S.
　1974　　　　Obedience to Authority.　New York:
　　　　　　　Harper and Row.

Miller, D., Hintz, R., and Couch, C.
　1975　　　　"The Elements and Structure of Openings."
　　　　　　　In Couch and Hintz, (eds.).

Miller, D.
　1978　　　　"Methodological Procedures in Videotape
　　　　　　　Analysis."　Unpublished manuscript,
　　　　　　　University of Manitoba.

　1979　　　　The Structure and Process of Authority
　　　　　　　Relations: Hypnosis.　Unpublished
　　　　　　　Ph. D. dissertation, University of
　　　　　　　Iowa.

Miller, D.
　1973　　　　George Herbert Mead: Self, Language and
　　　　　　　World.　Chicago: University of Chicago
　　　　　　　Press.

Miller, S.
　1973　　　　"Ends, Means and Galumping: Some
　　　　　　　Leitmotifs of PLay."　American
　　　　　　　Anthropologist, LXXV: 88-99.

Miller, L.
　1972　　　　An Approach to PLay.　Unpublished M. A.
　　　　　　　thesis, University of Massachusetts at
　　　　　　　Amherst.

Mills, C. W.
　1940　　　　"Situated Actions and Vocabularies of
　　　　　　　Motives."　American Sociological Review,
　　　　　　　5: 904-913.

　1959　　　　The Sociological Imagination.　London:
　　　　　　　Oxford University Press.

Mohmann, G. P.
　1982　　　　"An Essay on Fantasy Theme Criticism."
　　　　　　　Quarterly Journal of Speech, 68: 109-132.

McHugh, P.
　1968　　　　Definition of the Situation.　Indianapolis:
　　　　　　　The Bobbs-Merrill Company, Inc. .

Neff, R.
1975   "Toward an Interactionist Theory of
            Social Structure." In Couch and Hintz
            (eds.).

Nichols, M. H.
1971   "Kenneth Burke and the New Rhetoric."
            in R. Johonsen (ed.). Contemporary
            Theories of Rhetoric: Selected Readings.

Ogden and Richards
1923   The Meaning of Meaning.New York:
            Harcourt, Brace and Company.

Orne, M.
1962   "On the Social Psychology ofPsychology
            Experiments: With Particular Reference to
            Demand Characteristics and Their
            Implications." American Psychologist,
            17: 776-783.

Perinbanaygam, R. S.
1974   "The Definition of the Situation:
            An Analysis of the Ethnomethodological
            and Dramaturgical View." Sociological
            Quarterly, 15: 521-541.

Pirandello, L.
1952   Naked Masks. New York: Dutton.

Scheff, T.
1970   "On the Concept of Identity and Social
            Relationships." in T. Shibutani, (ed.).

Scott
1955   "Reliability of Content Analysis: The Case
            of Nominal Scale Coding." Public Opinion
            Quarterly, Fall.

Scott and Lyman
1968   "Accounts." American Sociological Review,
            33: 46-62.

Searle, J.
1969   Speech Acts. New York: Cambridge
            University Press.

Sehested and Couch
1978   "Authoritarianism in the Small Group
          Laboratory." Unpublished manuscript,
          University of Iowa.

Schutz, A.
1968   The Phenomenology of the Social World.
          Evanston: Northwestern University Press.

Simmel, G.
1950   The Sociology of Georg Simmel. Wulff
          (ed.). New York: The Free Press.

Sink and Couch
1979   "Negotiating." Paper presented to the
          SSSI meetings.

Stebbins, R.
1972   "Studying the Definition of the Situation:
          Theory and Field Research Strategies."
          in Manis and Meltzer (eds.).

Stokes, R. and Hewitt, J.
1976   "Aligning Actions."American Sociological
          Review, 41: 838-849.

Stone and Faberman
1970   Social Psychology Through Symbolic
          Interaction. Waltham: Ginn-Biasdell.

Stover, S.
1974   "Notes on Context of Interaction: An
          Attempt at Convergence Between Cybernetics
          and Symbolic Interaction." Paper presented
          to the Midwest Sociological Association
          Meetings.

1978   "Context and Relationship." Paper to the
          Midwest Sociological Association Meetings.

Thomas, W. I.
1923   The Unadjusted Girl. Boston: Little,
          Brown and Company.

Thomas, W. I. and Swaine Thomas, D.
1928   The Child in America. New York: Alfred
          Knopf.

Travisano, R.
1975   "Comments on A Research Paradigm for
         Symbolic Interaction." in Couch and
         Hintz (eds.).

Turner, R.
1953   "The Quest for Universals in Sociological
         Research." American Sociological Review,
         24: 605-611.

1962   "Role-taking: Process Versus Conformity."
         in Rose, A. (ed.). Human Behavior and
         Social Process. Boston: Houghton-Mifflin
         Co. .

Van Dijk, T.
1977   "Context and Cognition: Knowledge Frames
         and Speech Act Comprehension."Journal
         of Pragmatics, 1: 211-232.
Waller, W.
1970   "The Definition of the Situation." in
         Stone and Faberman (eds.).

Watzlawick, P., Beavin, J. and Jackson
1967   Pragmatics of Human Communication.
         New York: Norton.

Weiland, M.
1975   "Forms of Social Relationships." in
         Couch and Hintz (eds.).

Wenzel, J.
1979   "Jurgen Habermas and the Dialectical
         Perspective on Argument" Journal of the
         American Forensic Association, vol. 16,
         Fall.

Wilson, T.
1976   "Normative and Interpretive Paradigms in
         Sociology." in Douglas (ed.).
         Understanding Everyday Life.

Winnicott, D. W.
1971   Playing and Reality. New York:
         Basic Books.

Wrong, D.
1976   Skeptical Sociology. New York: Columbia
            University Press.

Wuthrow, Hunter, Bergesen and Kurzweil
    1984   Cultural Analysis. Boston: Routledge and
            Kegan Paul.

Zimmermann, D.
    1979   "Ethnomethodology and Symbolic Interaction:
            Some Reflections on Natruralistic Inquiry."
            Paper presented to the SSSI meetings.

APPENDIX A

TRANSCRIPTS OF
FANCIFUL RECONTEXTUALIZATION
EPISODES

Mary:
   (looks down at own papers)
Gail: Shoot! Now let's see (pause) what's the best
   (looks down at own papers, voice softens)
Lois:
   (looks down at own papers)
Anne:
   (looks down at own papers)

Mary:

Gail: way of doing this?   Sometimes it just,uh, read

Lois:

Anne:

Mary: Yeah.

Gail: off the numbers and filling them in?

Lois: Yeah!

Anne:

Mary:

Gail:

Lois: That's what we have to do first (pause)   Oh

Anne:

Mary:

Gail:

Lois: Lord! Spare us (pause)   Don't look at yourself
                                  (looks over at A)
Anne:
                                  (starts rummaging

Mary:

Gail:

Lois: on television (snickers).
       (nudges A with elbow)
Anne: I'm trying to get this
          through purse)

Mary:

Gail:

Lois:

Anne: (pause) I'm going to get this ugly blue bag

Mary:

Gail:

Lois: out of your, off of, out of, I
Anne: out of here, because, because

Mary: You
                    (looks at A, is drinking
Gail:

Lois: thought she was going to say off of her eyes.

Anne:
       (puts purse on lap and continues to rummage

Mary: start doing this. . .putting on make-up
       coffee) (rubs underneath own eyes)
Gail:

Lois:

Anne:
       through it)

```
Mary:   (laughs)

Gail:   (laughs)
        (looks at L)
Lois:   (laughs)  And it's just her pocketbook.
                  (mock hits A)
Anne:                                            I hate
                                                 (puts

Mary:

Gail:

Lois:         Get that away from here.  All right.

Anne:   it.
        purse on table off camera)

Mary:           *  For someone with MRS on their sweater
                   (looks at A, then L)      (EC=L)
Gail:

Lois:   All right.
        (looks at papers in front of her) (EC=M)
Anne:
                            (covers MRS with hand)

Mary:           It's embarrassing!

Gail:     MRS?
          (looks at A's sweater)
Lois:   MRS!

Anne:                           My degree I'm after,
                                (points at MRS on her

Mary:

Gail:                           Oh, yeah, right.

Lois:

Anne:   MRS., my MRS. degree.
        sweater)
```

Mary:

Gail: What's your fisrt name? Oh, that's right, we

Lois: M. S-------- R---! What's M?

Anne: Mary.
                       (looks at G)

Mary: That's

Gail: talked about that. From the soap opera.
              (looks at A)

Lois: I forgot
                        (drinks

Anne: soap opera.

Mary: just what I was thinking.

Gail: Oh, except Mary Ryan's
               (looks down at papers)

Lois: about that.
      coffee)

Anne:

Mary:

Gail: dead.

Lois: She's dead (pause) well, um, this says MRS,
      (puts down coffee, looks at A, reaches over

Anne:

Mary: (laughs)

Gail: (laughs)

Lois: what do you think that means? (laughs)
      points at MRS initials)

Anne: (laughs) I'll

Mary: (laughs)

Gail: (laughs)

Lois: (laughs) Okay. We don't

Anne: just get a masters now. (laughs)

Mary:

Gail:

Lois: have to make all of the X's since we did them

Anne:

Mary: the

Gail:

Lois: all together. We just have to read off

Anne:

Mary: numbers, shall I go first?

Gail:

Lois:

Anne:

* This line of conversation indicates the beginning of
Episode #2.

188

Mary: "Writes Articulately" 3-1-6
     (writing and looking down at own papers)
Gail:
     (writing and looking down at own papers)
Lois:
     (writing and looking down at own papers)
Anne: Oh, that's what it
     (writing and looking down at own papers)

Mary:

Gail:

Lois: No, that's not what it says.   "Writing and
     (looks up at M)   (looks at A)
Anne: says.   "Writing and

Mary: Oh, okay I put 3-1-6

Gail: Oh.   3-1-6

Lois: Articulating"   3-1-6

Anne: Articulating"   3-1-6

Mary: (laughs)   (laughs)

Gail: (laughs)   (laughs)
     (puts head down on table)
Lois: (laughs) I made a big deal out of that (laughs)
        (gestures at the air)   (looks at G)
Anne: (laughs)   (laughs)

Mary:

Gail:

Lois: No! It 's not writing and articulating, Mary,
     (raises voice mockingly, looks at M, pounds
Anne:

Mary:

Gail:

Lois: you jerk! You're screwing up the intercoder
       fist on table)
Anne:

Mary: And it's the only one on the page
                         (looks at L)
Gail:

Lois: reliability (laughs)   on the page
                                                (looks at G)
Anne:
                                 (looks at M)

Mary: that we all agree on.   No.

Gail: It is, isn't it?
                             (looks down at papers in
Lois: that we got right.   No. 2, 2, 2

Anne: No. 2 others.

Mary:

Gail: Where are they?   Friendly
        front of her)
Lois: others.   Yeah.

Anne: listening.

Mary: Clarity, and yeah, ones that have come
                             (makes circular
Gail: Attitude.

Lois:

Anne:

```
Mary:   up on every questionnaire (laugh)
        gesture with hands, looks at L)
Gail:                                    There
                                         (points
Lois:                            Where?
                         (looks down at papers)
Anne:


Mary:

Gail:   they are.
        at L's papers)
Lois:          That's right.

Anne:
```

Mary: Oh My God,
                                    (looks at L)
Gail:

                                    (looks at M)
Lois:
        (YAWNS EXAGGERATELY, PUTS HAND OVER MOUTH)
Anne:
          (writing on papers in front of her)

Mary: I'm going to have to erase it from the tape

Gail:

Lois:

Anne:

Mary: (pause)   Subject number 2 yawns.
                  (teasing voice)
Gail: (laughing) Subject #1 is
                              (looks at L, leans
Lois:

Anne:

Mary: Is waving (pause)

Gail: looking at herself.   Can I Say
        forward) (looks at L)
Lois: (laughing) Hi Mom.
        (tries to see self in t.v. moniter) (waves at
Anne:
          (continues writing)

Mary: I had a friend who worked in all of our

Gail:

Lois:

        camera)
Anne:
          (looks up at M and then G)

                        192

Mary: experiments, and um, for his masters thesis

Gail:

Lois:

Anne:

Mary: he wrote on reactivity to the camera, so he had

Gail:

Lois:

Anne:

Mary: all of these transcripts with people: "hi mom,"

Gail:

Lois:

Anne:

Mary: or grabbing the microphone so that we couldn't

Gail:

Lois:

Anne:

Mary: hear what they were planning to do to conspire,

Gail:

Lois:

Anne:

```
Mary:    it was great.
         (voice trails off)
Gail:
         (picks up coffee)
Lois:      I'm not reactive to the microphone at all)
         (looks at microphone, puts head close to talk)
Anne:
         (looking at papers in front of her)

Mary:

Gail:    * Aw, I'm sad.

Lois:                    Well, G, you don't look sad, you
                        (looks at G, sits back in chair,
Anne:


Mary:

Gail:
                                           (makes sad
Lois:    don't have the E and F universal affect
         shuffles papers, makes face, looks at A, then
Anne:


Mary:                           What are you suppose to do?
                                (makes face at L and A)
Gail:
         face, looks at L)
Lois:    display.
         M)
Anne:            Don't be sad.
                (looks at G, makes sad face).


Mary:

Gail:    Happy!
         (makes face, looks at L and A)
Lois:              Startled!                 Fear!
                  (makes face, positions arms)  (makes
Anne:    (laughs)                  (laughs)
         (looks at M)              (looks at L)
```

194

Mary:

Gail:

Lois: I can't get
      fearful face)
Anne: Little round mouth for surprise.
      (looks at G, makes circle with hand)

Mary:

Gail:

Lois: that one. Oh, she's good. Oh, now that's
                        (looks at m)
Anne:

Mary:

Gail: (laughs)
                (makes surprised face)
Lois: coquettish.

Anne: (laughs)   Oh, that's good. You've probably
                 (looks at G)

Mary: (laughs)
                            (hits head with
Gail: Definitely (laughs) High reliability.

Lois:

Anne: been trained.

Mary: Is that what you
      hand)   (looks at G)
Gail: I can get it on the non-verbals.

Lois:

Anne:

```
Mary:   teach your students?

Gail:                           Honest.
                        (makes serious face)
Lois:                                   Question 7.
            (looks at G and then M)
Anne:                               Surprise.
              (looks at G, makes face)

Mary:   OHHHH!   1-1-4

Gail:                               3-1-4

Lois:                       3-1-4

Anne:                   1-1-4
```

* Episode #4 begins with this line of text.

```
Mary:    Okay, "listens," 1-2-3
         (looks down at papers in front of her)
Gail:                                   3-2-1
         (looks down at papers in front of her)
Lois:                          1-2-3
         (looks down at papers in front of her)
Anne:                          1-2-3
         (looks down at papers in front of her)


Mary:
         (leand back in chair, looks at G)
Gail:    (laughs)                       Sorry (laughing

Lois:             What! Are you serious?

Anne:
         (leans back in chair, looks at G)

Mary:

Gail:    very hard)  I just couldn't resist.   It's the
                             · (looks down at papers,
Lois:

Anne:


Mary:             I was just going to say, it happened. IT

Gail:    same.
         shakes head, No)
Lois:

Anne:


Mary:    HAPPENED!

Gail:    (continues laughing)

Lois:                           It happened, the dummy
                                (looks down at own papers)
Anne:
```

```
Mary:                    Point to the loon. "Tries to help,"

Gail:            (laughs)
                 (looks down at own papers)
Lois:   emereged. (laughs)

Anne:            (laughs)


Mary:  1-2-5

Gail:                              1-2-5

Lois:                  1-2-5

Anne:          1-2-5
```

Mary: "Tries to put self in others situation" 1-2-5
        (reading from papers in front of her)
Gail:
        (looking at papers in front of her)
Lois:
        (looking at papers in front of her)
Anne:
        (looking at papers in front of her)

Mary:

Gail: No, I
                                    (looks
Lois: 1-2-5
          (EC=A)
Anne: 1-2-3   um, well, being understood
        (EC=L) (looks at G, gestures with hands)

Mary: Yeah, taking the role of the other
           (looks down at own papers)
Gail: think so   Yeah
     at A)
Lois:
                                  (looks
Anne:

Mary:

Gail: I said 1-2-5 but if you're going to talk about
           (EC=A)
Lois:
     down at own papers)
Anne:
          (EC=G)

Mary:

Gail: reception skills empathy is considered one in

Lois:

Anne:

Mary:

Gail: the literature, I mean I coded it 1-2-5 'cause

Lois:

Anne:
                                                    (looks

Mary:
                                        (looks at G)
Gail: I made reception skills very narrow, but we've
                                                    (looks at
Lois:

Anne:
        at G and then M)

Mary:
                                        (looks down at own
Gail: got a real problem with this category in terms
        M)   (looks down at own
Lois:
                                        (looks down at own
Anne:
                                        (looks down at own

Mary: Yeah, um 'cause if you read it as
        papers)
Gail: of definition
        papers)
Lois:
        papers)
Anne:
        papers)

Mary: sensitive it can

Gail:

Lois: No, no, it doesn't say
                                (looking down at own
Anne:
                                (looking down at own

200

Mary:

Gail: But if you can put yourself

Lois: sensitive (pause)
        papers)
Anne:
        papers)

Mary:

Gail: in the role of the other

Lois: But it says tries to
                               (reading from own papers)
Anne:

Mary:

Gail: That's putting
                               (looks at L)
Lois: put self in others situation

Anne:

Mary:

Gail: yourself in the role of the other.

Lois: No, I
                                         (looks up at
Anne:
                                         (looks at G

Mary:

Gail:

Lois: understand but when we said a reception skill
        M, then G)
Anne:
        and then L)

201

Mary:

Gail:

Lois: presumably that's something that's going on

Anne:

Mary:

Gail: huh, um but
                                                (looks at L)
Lois: during the communication process

Anne:

Mary:
                                 (EC=G)
Gail: don't you use empathy during the communication
                                 (EC=M)
Lois:

Anne:

Mary:

Gail: process?

Lois: Well, you can say empathy but you can

Anne:

Mary: Yeah, I'm sure this
                                    (EC=A, smiles)
Gail:

Lois: have empathy outside of the

Anne:
                                    (EC=M, smiles)

Mary: person isn't thinking about it in terms of

Gail:

Lois:

Anne:

Mary: George Herbert Mead's definition of the meaning

Gail:

Lois:

Anne:

Mary: of the word.

Gail: But I can have great sensitivity
                         (EC=L)
Lois:
                         (EC=G)
Anne:

Mary:

Gail: toward the needs of others outside of the

Lois:

Anne:

Mary:

Gail: communication system too, I mean, I have great

Lois:

Anne:

Mary:
                  (looks at G)
Gail: sensitivity toward the starving children of the

Lois:

Anne:
                        (looks at G)

Mary: (laugh)

Gail: world (laugh) but I don't communicate with
                  (looks down at own papers)
Lois: (laugh)
                (looks at G)
Anne: (laugh)
                (looks at G)

Mary: (laughing) And you don't send them your

Gail: them (laughing)

Lois: (laughing)

Anne: (laughing)

Mary: dinner leftovers or cry when. . .

Gail: (laughing)

Lois: (laughing) I don't think you have any

Anne: (laughing)

Mary:

Gail:

Lois: sensitivity toward the starving children of the
                        (looks at A)
Anne:

Mary: How many starving children do you
          (looks at G, EC=G)
Gail:
                         (EC=M)
Lois: world.

Anne:

Mary: support?

Gail:

Lois:

Anne: I, I put it there because understanding
          (looking through own papers)

Mary:

Gail:

Lois:

Anne: is one of the reception skills so if . . .

Mary: Okay, (pause) tries to out talk others (laughs)

Gail: (laughs)

Lois: (laughs)

Anne: (laughs)

Mary:

Gail:

Lois: What, what? (laughs) I,uh, I uh, none of us

Anne:

Mary:

Gail:

Lois: knows how to out talk anyone. Anyone who

Anne:

Mary:

Gail:

Lois: wants to say anything, they can just say

Anne:

Mary:

Gail:

Lois: anything they want to say and we won't try to

Anne:

Mary:

Gail:

Lois: stop talking, anyone else, and if you have a

Anne:

Mary:

Gail:

Lois: point to make, you can just make your point

Anne:

Mary: (laugh)

Gail: (laugh)

Lois: and talk on, it doesn't (laugh) No one!

Anne: ·   (laugh)

Mary: (laughs)

Gail: (laughs).

Lois: interrupts (laughs) or talks over, or anything

Anne: (laughs)

Mary:

Gail:

Lois: like that. They just take their turns politely

Anne:

```
Mary:  (laughs)

Gail:  (laughs)                                    It's my

Lois:  (laughs)              The way they should.

Anne:  (laughs)  Turn-taking.


Mary:                    2-2-7          Yeah.

Gail:  turn.                    2-2-7?     Uhh!!

Lois:         It's M's turn.  3-2-7

Anne:  It's my turn, 2-2-7


Mary:

Gail:  Now, 2-2-7. Now I want you to think about this.

Lois:

Anne:


Mary:                                    Think of the

Gail:  Who tries to out talk other people?

Lois:

Anne:                                    Typically.


Mary:  physical attribrutes of those who try to out

Gail:  (laughs)

Lois:         Men? I'll change that.

Anne:
```

Mary: talk others.

Gail: And their organ-communication.

Lois:

Anne:

Mary: (laughs)

Gail: (laughs)

Lois: (laughs) Obviously, I had some problems

Anne: (laughs)

Mary: Two-organs. (laughs)

Gail: (laughs) Excuse me!

Lois: conceptualizing. (laughs) What? Well we san

Anne: (laughs)

Mary:

Gail:

Lois: probably do that part better when A comes back

Anne:

Mary:

Gail:

Lois: from Purdue where they study ORGAN COMM

Anne: Dear God!!

```
Mary:   (laughs)                                    2-1-6 TOO
Gail:   (laughs)  Whoo!!! "Too Organized."
Lois:   (laughs)
Anne:   (laughs)


Mary:   ORGAN-ized
Gail:                                      3-1-6
Lois:                            3-1-6
Anne:                  3-1-6
```

Mary: If you look at the list of all of the bad or
         (looks down at papers)
Gail:
         (looks down at papers)
Lois:
          (looks down at papers)
Anne:
         (looks down at papers)

Mary: negative characteristics are coded female.

Gail: Yeah,
                                               (serious
Lois:

Anne:

Mary:

Gail: women are sorry creatures who lack skills but
         sounding voice, looks at L, EC=L)
Lois:
                                (EC=G)
Anne:

Mary: (laughs) That's what it sounds
                                 (leans back in chair,
Gail: who give of themselves (laughs)
                                 (looks at M)
Lois: (laughs)

Anne: (laughs)

Mary: like you. . .
         looks at G and then L)
Gail:

Lois: Women are (pause) we'll write it,
                                 (looks at m)
Anne:
         (looks down at own papers)

211

Mary: That

Gail:

Lois: this in our paper. Women are sorry creatures

Anne:

Mary: should be the first line in the introduction
      (continues looking at L)
Gail:

Lois:

Anne:

Mary: (laughs)

Gail:

Lois:

Anne: (laughs) Women are (pause) and we have evidence

Mary: This is
                                       (looks
Gail:

Lois: (laughs)   Yes we can prove that.
                         (looks down at own papers)
Anne: to prove it (laughs)

Mary: research done by women, so, of course, sexism
      down at own papers)
Gail:

Lois:

Anne:

Mary: can't be an issue

Gail: be an issue, right, sexist? me?
                   (looks down at own papers)
Lois:

Anne:

Mary: Women aren't sexist (laughs) right.

Gail: (laughs)

Lois: (laughs)

Anne: (laughs) Uhh, okay, so
                                            (looks down at

Mary:

Gail:

Lois:

Anne: we had done. . .   ·
      own papers)

Mary:

Gail: But since fun to talk to is modified by our,um,

Lois:

Anne:

Mary:

Gail: by our happy disposition, that makes it female,

Lois:

Anne:

Mary:

Gail: to me, I mean, people who have happy

Lois:

Anne:

Mary: (laughs)

Gail: dispositions are women (laughs)

Lois: (laughs) I don't have

Anne: (laughs)

. Mary:

Gail: I mean there are agreeable

Lois: any problem with that

Anne:

Mary:

Gail: men and there are happy men, but when ypu think

Lois:

Anne:

Mary:

Gail: of happy disposition, the stereotype is the

Lois:

Anne:

Mary:

Gail: chipper little housewife

Lois: Housewife, that's the female,

Anne:

Mary:

Gail: Huh, when I was seventeen a woman

Lois: I'll buy that.

Anne:

Mary:

Gail: told me I'd never find a husband unless I

Lois:

Anne:

Mary: (spits) What a crock of shit!

Gail: learned to smile.

Lois:

Anne:

Mary: (laughs)   (laughs)

Gail: (laughs) Awright, (laughs) From

Lois: She was right. (laughs)   (laughs)

Anne: (laughs)   (laughs)

Mary: to smile (laughs)

Gail: that moment on I vowed never to smile (laughs)

Lois: (laughs)

Anne: (laughs)

Mary: By smiling?

Gail: But that's how she met her husband.   No

Lois:

Anne:

Mary:

Gail: because he liked her because she smiled all

Lois:

Anne:

Mary:

Gail: the time, and dear, if you wish to find

Lois:

Anne:

Mary: Yeah, you can go out on the

Gail: someone to like you.

Lois:

Anne:

Mary: street corner and

Gail:

Lois: Yeah, and use the odd socks

Anne:

Mary:

Gail: Oh the review, no not the review,

Lois: routine (laughs)

Anne: (laughs)

Mary:

Gail: the review with E----- H-----, when I was

Lois:

Anne:

217

Mary:

Gail: reading about the play OF PLENTY, yeah, the odd

Lois: I'm sorry. I didn't see you there.
       (accidently kicks A under table)
Anne:

Mary:

Gail: socks routine. The absent-minded professor is

Lois:

Anne:

Mary: (laughs)

Gail: extremely sexy to women (laughs)

Lois: (laughs) The absent-

Anne: (laughs)

Mary:

Gail: So we must all be in love with V---.

Lois: minded man, you know, like he meets his wife,

Anne:

Mary: (laughs)

Gail: (laughs)

Lois: like he convinces his wife, he wins her by

Anne:

Mary: Oh, so oh,

Gail:

Lois: wearing odd colored socks, you know so she'd

Anne: someone to

Mary: that's disgusting when you think about it.

Gail:

Lois: The

Anne: take care of him

Mary:

Gail:

Lois: odd socks routine. So happy disposition is

Anne:

Mary:

Gail: It was a male writing the article so you

Lois: female.

Anne:

Mary: He wears odd socks.   (laughs)

Gail: know, uh, it was probably a male myth.

Lois: (laughs)

Anne: (laughs)

219

```
Mary:                                        (laughs)
                                            (throws head
Gail:                                        (laughs)
                                            (claps hands
Lois:     "Lets people make fun of her."    (laughs) Yeah!

Anne:                              A fool!     (laughs)


Mary:                                          (laughs)
          back, looks at A)
Gail:     Well, we know it's a woman, right.! (laughs)
          looks at A)
Lois:                                          (laughs)

Anne:                                          (laughs) A


Mary:                  (laughs)  A real Wo-man (laughs)
                             (looks down at own papers)
Gail:                 (laughs)                     Oh
                             (looks down at own papers)
Lois:                 (laughs)
                             (looks down at own papers)
Anne:     true woman.  (laughs)
                             (looks down at own papers)

Mary:

Gail:     that's also what we're going to include, a

Lois:

Anne:
                   (looks up at G)

Mary:

Gail:     section in our paper on real women (laughs) in

Lois:

Anne:
```

Mary:

Gail: fact we could write a book: Real Women Let

Lois:

Anne:

Mary: Smile A Lot

Gail: People Make Fun of Them,

Lois: No, real

Anne:

Mary:

Gail:

Lois: women don't smile (laughs) real women don't

Anne:

Mary: (laughs)
       (looks at L)
Gail: (laughs)
        (looks at L)
Lois: listen, real women   (laughs)

Anne: real women are men. (laughs)

Mary: I coded it. . .
              (looks down at own papers)
Gail:
              (looks down at own papers)
Lois: Oh dear! "Lets people make fun of her."

Anne:

ABOUT THE AUTHOR

M. Nawal Lutfiyya holds a B.A. in Sociology and History from the University of Manitoba in Winnipeg, Canada; an M.A. in Sociology and Anthropology from the University of Iowa; and a Ph.D. in Communication from the University of Massachusetts at Amherst. She has taught at Marist College in Poughkeepsie, New York and currently teaches at the University of Louisville in Kentucky.